ONDORI

A NEW LOOK FOR NEEDLEWORK

Embroidery and Cr

MW01013023

CONTENTS

★Copyright © 1984 Ondorisha Publishers, Ltd., All Rights Reserved.
★Published by Ondorisha Publishers, Ltd.,
 11-11 Nishigoken-cho, Shinjuku-ku, Tokyo 162, Japan.
★Distributors:
●United States. Canada. The Far East and Japan
 Japan Pubrications Trading Co., Ltd.,
 1-2-1, Sarugaku-cho, Chiyoda-ku. Tokyo, 101 Japan.
 FAX:81-3-3292-0410, TEL:81-3-3292-3751
●United Kingdom and Europe:Premier Book Marketing Ltd.,
 1 Gower Street, London Wc1E 6HA
●Australia and New Zealand:Bookwise International,
 54 Crittenden Road, Findon, South Australia 5023
 10 9 8 7 6 5 4 3
★ISBN 0-87040-568-3
 Printed in Japan.

WELCOME TO MY HOUSE

Come to my house and breathe fresh country air.
Let's have tea and sit in the sun with our needlework.
I'll bake a cake full of the
fragrance of spring.

Bell Flower and Sweet Pea Tablecloth
Instructions on page 42.

Tree and House
Tablecloth
Instructions
on page 54.

Sofa Throw
Instructions on page 48.

6

Tree Cushion
Instructions on page 51.

Petite
Fleur Bouquet
Table Runner
Instructions
on page 58.

Country Scene Table Center
Instructions on page 63.

14

FOR MY PRINCE CHARMING

Eager for spring, I have made new curtains,
tablecloths, and napkins. When shall my prince come to
share my table?

Lace-insert Curtain, Cushions, Tablecloth and Napkins
Instructions on page 90.

Country House
Table Center,
Matching Curtain
and Cushion

Personal Mug
Placemats and
Tray Mat

Instructions
for Curtain,
Cushion and
Table Center
on page 74,
and for Tray Mat
and Placemats
on page 77.

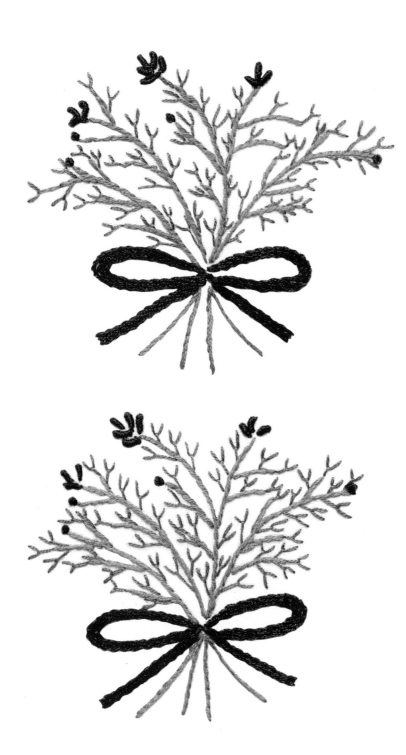

SMALL PICTURES

Small pictures to embroider and
hang on your walls
add a lovely and delightful touch
to your room.

Spring Scenes Instructions on page 66.

WELCOME TO MY HOUSE

FLOWERBASKET

Flower Garden Picture
Instructions on page 87.

Wall Hanging with Pockets
Instructions on page 70.

BEAUTIFUL DREAMS

Stitch your dreams into these romantic pillow cases and bedspreads.
They'll add a cheerful touch to your bedroom.

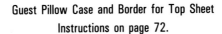

Guest Pillow Case and Border for Top Sheet
Instructions on page 72.

Floral
Bedspread
Instructions
on page 79.

Village
Bedspread
Instructions
on page 100.

LIVING WITH EMBROIDERY

Add a personal touch to ready-made shirts and aprons.
Embroidery brings color and charm to your life.

T-shirts Instructions on page 98.

Happy Birthday

Patchwork Tea Cozy and Toaster Cover Instructions on page 84.

Vegetable Placemats and Coasters
Instructions for Placemats on page 93 and for Coasters on page 95.

Tote Bags
Instructions on page 109.

39

Toilet Paper Holder and Doorknob Covers
Instructions for Toilet Paper Holder on page 96
and for Doorknob Covers on page 97.

ꟼNSTRUCTIONS

You've watered the forget-me-nots by the window
and had pancakes and coffee for breakfast.
Now another wonderful day begins.
Get your favorite embroidery thread and fabric and set to work.

Bell Flower and Sweet Pea Tablecloth   Shown on page 1.

FABRIC: Unbleached Irish linen, 137cm square.
THREADS: Anchor 6-strand embroidery floss:
5 skeins of Moss Green (265); 3 skeins each of Soft Pink (73),
Green (262); 2 skeins each of Almond Green (208); Forget-me-not
Blue (144, 130); 1-1/2 skeins each of Magenta Rose (48, 52),
Morocco Red (49); 1 skein each of Saffron (291), Magenta Rose
(41), Pistachio Green (242), Cornflower Blue (130).

FINISHED SIZE: 126cm square.
DIRECTIONS: Match triangles △ and circles ⊙, and transfer
design to fabric. Embroider. Turn edges back twice and fix hem
in place with modified closed buttonhole stitch on right side,
mitering corners (see page 45).

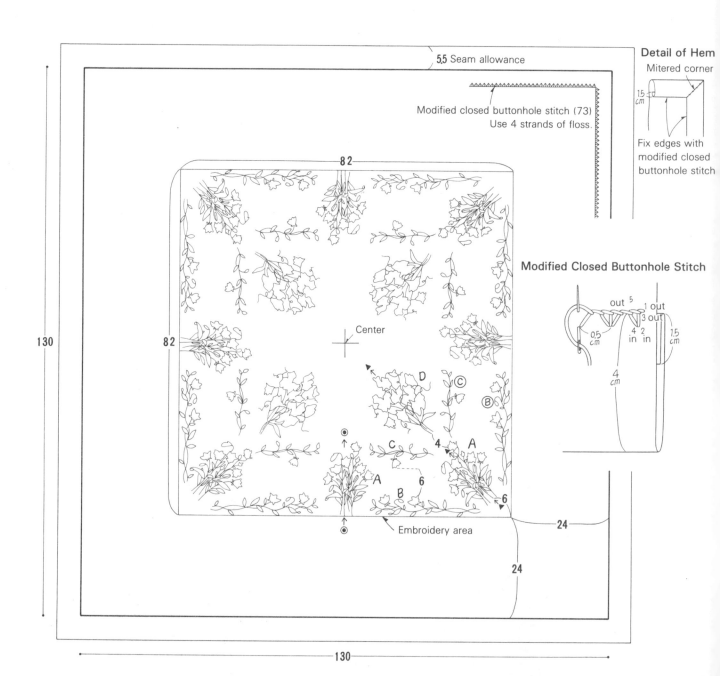

5.5 Seam allowance

Modified closed buttonhole stitch (73)
Use 4 strands of floss.

Detail of Hem
Mitered corner
1.5 cm
Fix edges with
modified closed
buttonhole stitch

82

82

Center

130

D ©C
     ®B
C   4   A
A   6
  B   6
Embroidery area

Modified Closed Buttonhole Stitch
out 5 1 out
         3 out
0.5 cm   4 2
         in in   1.5 cm
    4 cm

24

24

130

42

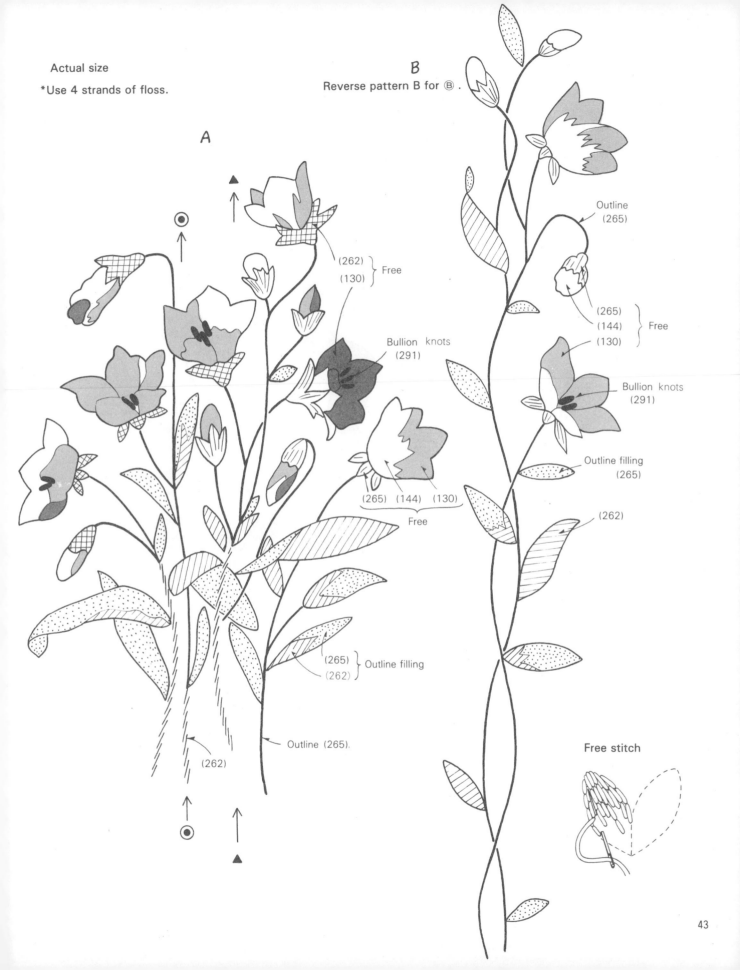

Actual size

*Use 4 strands of floss.

A

B

Reverse pattern B for ⓑ .

(262)
(130) } Free

Bullion knots
(291)

(265)
(144) } Free
(130)

(265) (144) (130)
Free

(265)
(262) } Outline filling

Outline (265).

(262)

Outline
(265)

(265)
(144) } Free
(130)

Bullion knots
(291)

Outline filling
(265)

(262)

Free stitch

43

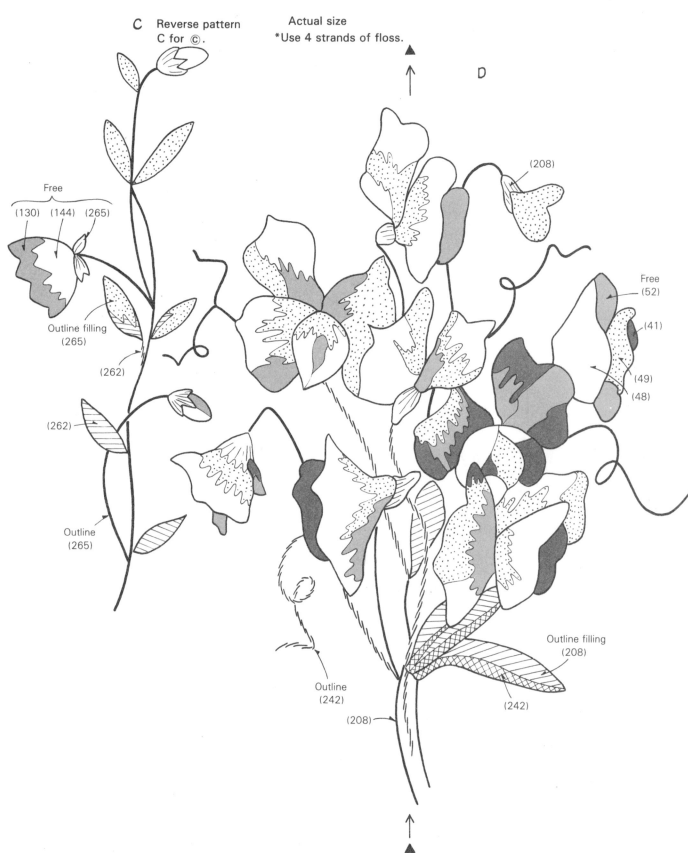

C **Reverse pattern**
C for ⓒ.

Actual size
*Use 4 strands of floss.

D

(208)

Free
(52)

(41)

(49)

(48)

Free
(130) (144) (265)

Outline filling
(265)

(262)

(262)

Outline
(265)

Outline filling
(208)

(242)

Outline
(242)

(208)

44

Cross-Stitch Tablecloth   Shown on pages 2 and 3.

FABRIC: Beige Java canvas (35 threads to 10cm), 91cm by 328cm.

THREADS: DMC 6-strand embroidery floss:
9 skeins of Drab (613); 4 skeins each of Geranium Red (892), Peony Rose (956); 3 skeins each of Scarab Green (3347), Geranium Pink (893), Pistachio Green (320); 2-1/2 skeins of Geranium Pink (894); 2 skeins each of Emerald Green (954), Tangerine Yellow (743); 1-1/2 skeins each of Cerise (600), Raspberry Red (3688), Parma Violet (209, 208), White; 1 skein each of Cerise (602), Raspberry Red (3689), Episcopal Purple (718), Parma Violet (211); Forget-me-not Blue (799), Laurel Green (988), Dark Brown (3033), Drab (612); 1/2 skein of Sèvres Blue (800).

FINISHED SIZE: 152cm by 113cm.

DIRECTIONS: Cut fabric. Cross-stitch as indicated. Join fabric pieces to make one piece 125cm by 164cm. Turn edges back twice and hemstitch on one side, mitering corners.

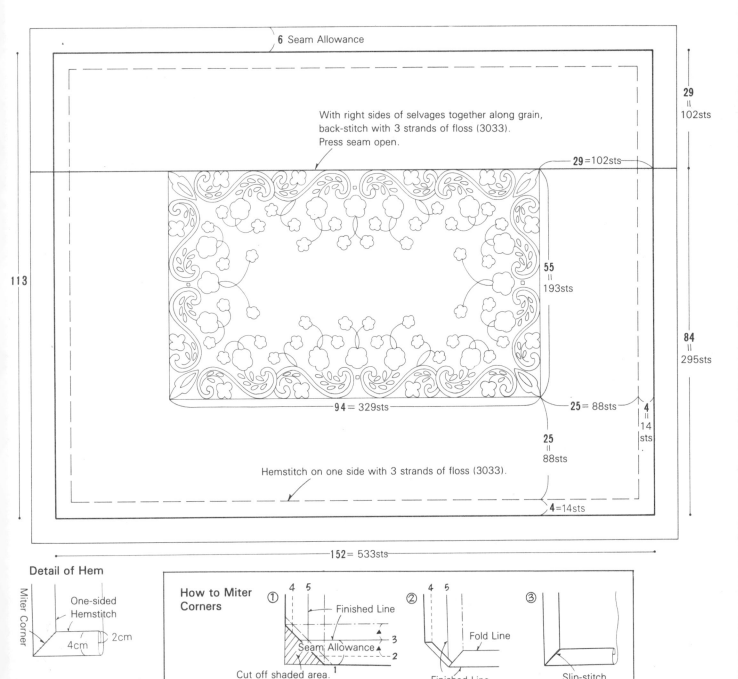

6 Seam Allowance

With right sides of selvages together along grain, back-stitch with 3 strands of floss (3033). Press seam open.

29 = 102sts

29 = 102sts

55 = 193sts

113

84 = 295sts

94 = 329sts

25 = 88sts

4 = 14sts

25 = 88sts

Hemstitch on one side with 3 strands of floss (3033).

4 = 14sts

152 = 533sts

Detail of Hem

Miter Corner

One-sided Hemstitch

4cm   2cm

How to Miter Corners

① Cut off shaded area. Finished Line Seam Allowance 4 5 3 2 1

② Fold Line Finished Line 4 5

③ Slip-stitch

Fold fabric in numerical order from 1 to 5.

45

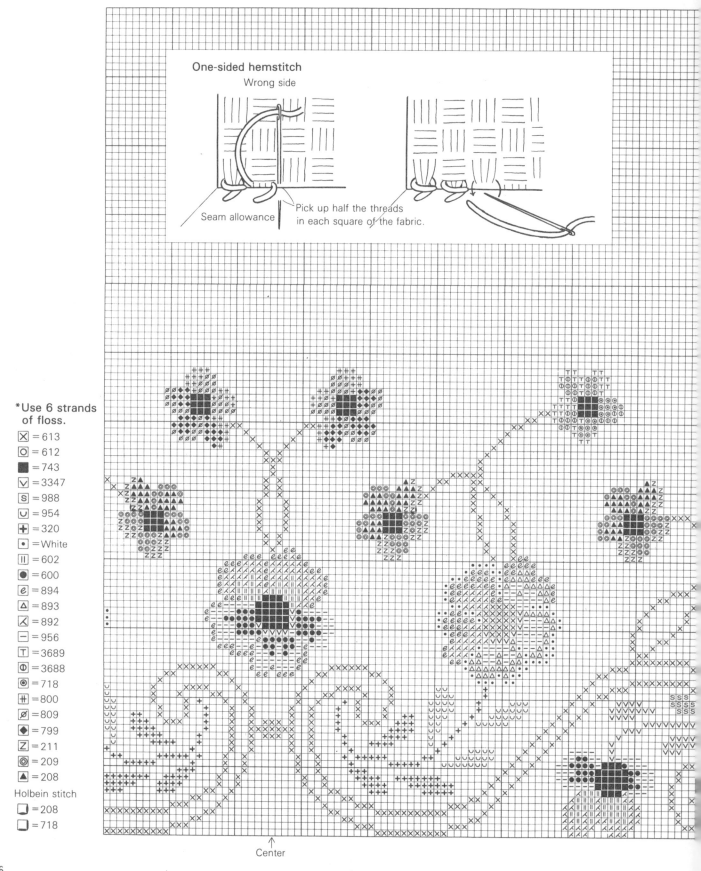

One-sided hemstitch

Wrong side

Seam allowance

Pick up half the threads
in each square of the fabric.

*Use 6 strands
  of floss.

X = 613
O = 612
■ = 743
V = 3347
S = 988
U = 954
+ = 320
• = White
‖ = 602
● = 600
e = 894
△ = 893
✕ = 892
— = 956
T = 3689
Φ = 3688
◉ = 718
+ = 800
Ø = 809
◆ = 799
Z = 211
◎ = 209
▲ = 208

Holbein stitch

▢ = 208
▢ = 718

Center

Center

One square of design equals one square mesh of fabric.

Sofa Throw   Shown on pages 6 and 7.

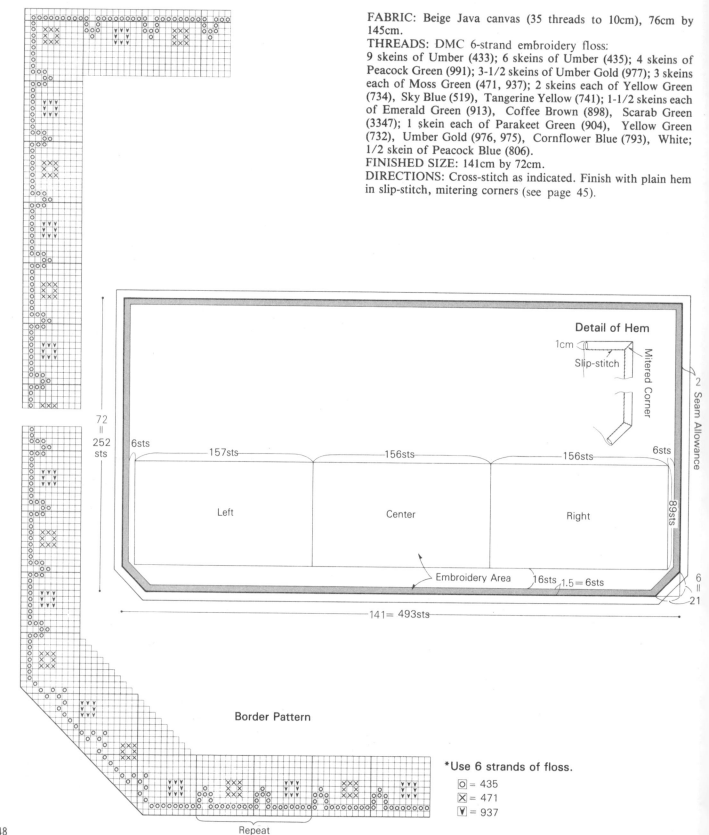

FABRIC: Beige Java canvas (35 threads to 10cm), 76cm by 145cm.

THREADS: DMC 6-strand embroidery floss:
9 skeins of Umber (433); 6 skeins of Umber (435); 4 skeins of Peacock Green (991); 3-1/2 skeins of Umber Gold (977); 3 skeins each of Moss Green (471, 937); 2 skeins each of Yellow Green (734), Sky Blue (519), Tangerine Yellow (741); 1-1/2 skeins each of Emerald Green (913), Coffee Brown (898), Scarab Green (3347); 1 skein each of Parakeet Green (904), Yellow Green (732), Umber Gold (976, 975), Cornflower Blue (793), White; 1/2 skein of Peacock Blue (806).

FINISHED SIZE: 141cm by 72cm.

DIRECTIONS: Cross-stitch as indicated. Finish with plain hem in slip-stitch, mitering corners (see page 45).

Detail of Hem

1cm

Slip-stitch

Mitered Corner

2 Seam Allowance

72 = 252 sts

6sts

157sts   156sts   156sts   6sts

Left   Center   Right

89sts

Embroidery Area   16sts   1.5 = 6sts

141 = 493sts

6 = 21

Border Pattern

Repeat

*Use 6 strands of floss.

O	= 435
X	= 471
V	= 937

48

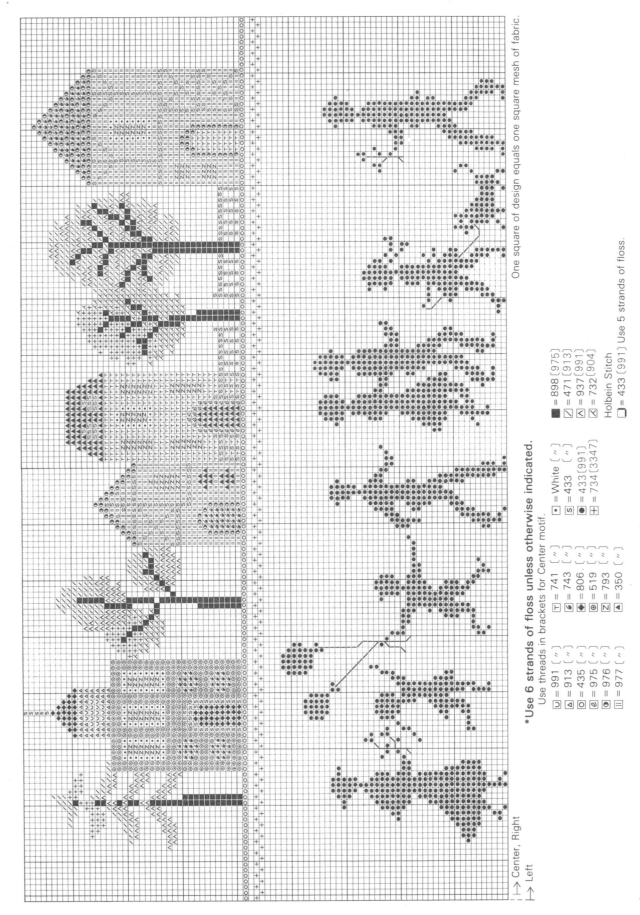

One square of design equals one square mesh of fabric.

↳→ Center, Right
↳→ Left

*Use 6 strands of floss unless otherwise indicated.
Use threads in brackets for Center motif.

U = 991 ["]	T = 741 ["]	• = White ["]	■ = 898 [975]
▲ = 913 ["]	▼ = 743 ["]	S = 433 ["]	Z = 471 [913]
O = 435 ["]	◆ = 806 ["]	● = 433[991]	< = 937[991]
⊘ = 975 ["]	Z = 519 ["]	+ = 734[3347]	X = 732[904]
◙ = 976 ["]	Z = 793 ["]		
⫴ = 977 ["]	▲ = 350 ["]		Holbein Stitch
			☐ = 433 [991] Use 5 strands of floss.

Floral Cushions Shown on page 8.

Fly stitch variation

out 3
1 out
2
in

3
5 / 4 in
out

out 7
6
in

Actual size
*Use 3 strands of floss.

Center

Outline
(258)

Long and
short { (330)
(323)

French knot   Straight

German knot

(302)   (334)

(258)

Outline
(255)

Satin (130)

French knot filling
(301)

Satin (334)

Fly variation
(211)

Open buttonhole
(330)   (302)

Satin
(255)

Satin
(258)

(211) { Fly
Lazy daisy

Long and short { (8)
(9)

(211) { Outline
Satin

(301)

Satin
(330)

French knot   Straight

(302)

Satin
(130)

Long and short
(9)

MATERIALS FOR ONE CUSHION
FABRIC: Cotton fabric; Cream for left cushion and Pistachio Green for right cushion, 90cm by 45cm each.
THREADS: Anchor 6-strand embroidery floss:
1 skein each of Scarab Green (255), Fire Red (334); 1/2 skein each of Morocco Red (9), Tangerine Yellow (323, 302, 301), Laurel Green (258), Cornflower Blue (130), Geranium Red (8,330), Peacock Green (211).

NOTIONS: 35cm zipper. 45cm square inner pillow stuffed with kapok.
FINISHED SIZE: 43cm square.
DIRECTIONS: Match centers of fabric and design, transfer design to 15.5cm diameter circle of front piece, and embroider. Sew zipper to back piece, sew front and back together with right sides facing, and turn inside out. Insert inner pillow.

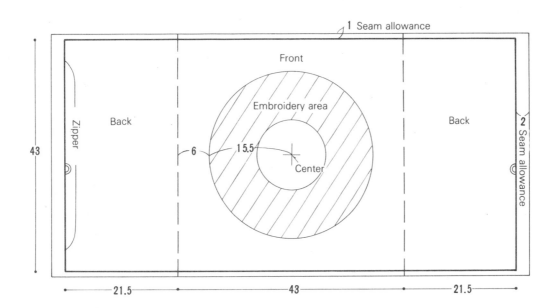

Tree Pillow   Shown on page 9.

FABRIC: Beige congress canvas (70 threads to 10cm), 91cm by 105cm.

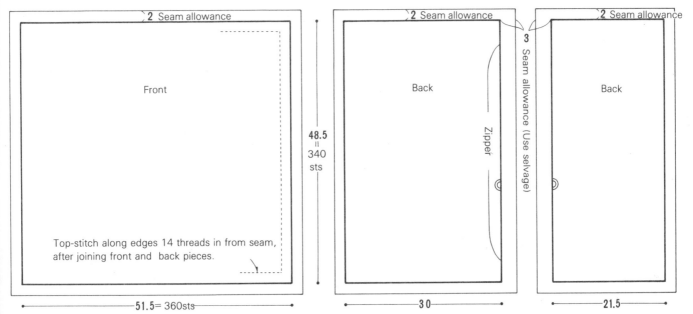

THREADS: DMC 6-strand embroidery floss:

16 skeins of Drab (610); 2 skeins each of Moss Green (469), Pistachio Green (320); 1-1/2 skeins each of Ash Gray (317), Green (3052), White; 1 skein each of Ash Gray (414), Moss Green (937), Green (3051), Dark Brown (3033), Beige (3047), Drab (613), Pistachio Green (369); 1/2 skein each of Pistachio Green (368), Sage Green (3012), Yellow Green (730), Smoke Gray (640), Drab (612), Raspberry Red (3688, 3689), Cerise (603); small amount each of Ash Gray (415, 318, 413), Moss Green (472, 470), Green (3053), Sage Green (3013), Cerise (604), Geranium Pink (893), Morocco Red (761), Magenta Rose (963), Saffron (726, 725, 727), Cornflower Blue (793), Indian Red (3041), Peacock Blue (807) and Greenish Gray (597).

NOTIONS: 40cm zipper. 50cm square inner pillow stuffed with kapok.

FINISHED SIZE: 51.5cm by 48.5cm.

*Use 6 strands of floss unless otherwise indicated.

🔲 = 415		☒ = 369	
☒ = 318		⊠ = 3053	
▲ = 414		▯ = 3052	
■ = 317		◉ = 3051	
● = 413		S = 3013	
△ = 472		Y = 3012	
⌷ = 470		T = 730	
V = 469		□ = 640	
⊞ = 937		C = 3047	
O = 368		✚ = 613	
◑ = 320		⊟ = 612	
Z = 3689		☒ = 610	
◤ = 3688		• = White	
T = 604		⊞ = 793	
E = 603		◆ = 3041	
Y = 893		⊟ = 807	
⊗ = 761		▯ = 597	
⊦ = 963			
⊠ = 726		Holbein stitch	
◇ = 725		◻ = 3033	
⊠ = 727		(Use 4 strands of floss)	
e = 3033			

Double cross-stitch

✳ = 610

(Use 9 strands of floss)

DIRECTIONS: Cut fabric. Cross-stitch as indicated. Sew zipper to back piece, sew front and back together with right sides facing, and turn inside out.

Top-stitch along edges 14 threads in from seam. Insert inner pillow.

Center

One square of design equals two-square mesh of fabric.

Tree and House Tablecloth   Shown on pages 4 and 5.

FABRIC: White Irish linen, 137cm by 180cm.
THREADS: Anchor 6-strand embroidery floss:
2 skeins of Smoke Gray (393); 1-1/2 skeins each of Scarab Green (255), Emerald Green (244); 1 skein each of Laurel Green (256), Canary Yellow (329), Geranium Pink (28); 1/2 skein each of Tangerine Yellow (303), Umber (370, 371), Sèvres Blue (131), and Parma Violet (110).
FINISHED SIZE: 176cm by 133cm.
DIRECTIONS: Transfer design to fabric as indicated. Embroider. Turn edges back twice and machine-stitch.

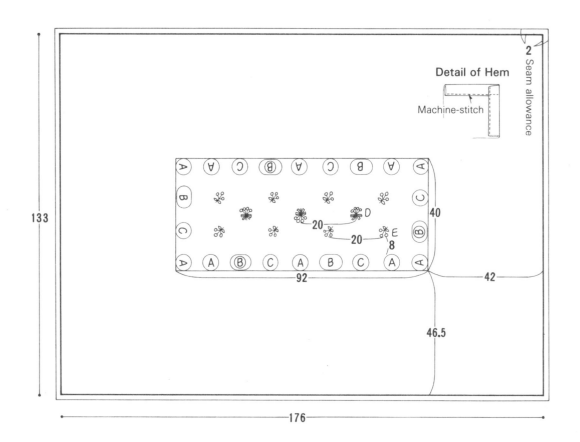

A   Actual size

B   Use (131) for Ⓑ instead of (28).

*Use 4 strands of floss unless otherwise indicated.

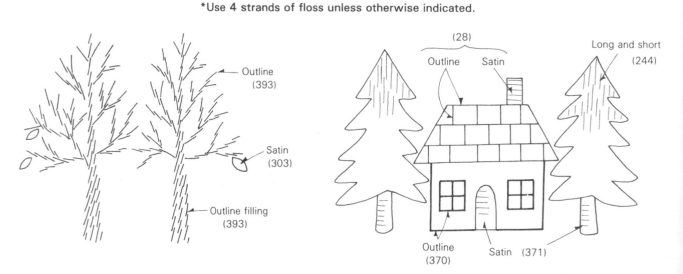

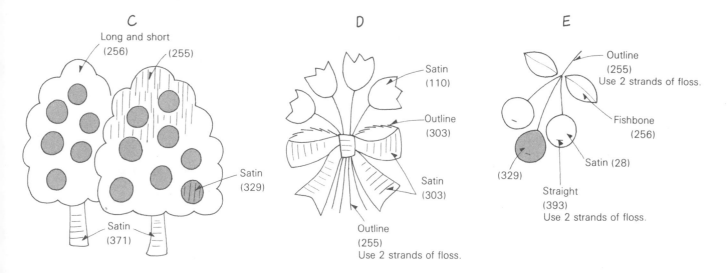

C

Long and short (256)

(255)

Satin (329)

Satin (371)

D

Satin (110)

Outline (303)

Satin (303)

Outline (255)
Use 2 strands of floss.

E

Outline (255)
Use 2 strands of floss.

Fishbone (256)

Satin (28)

(329)

Straight (393)
Use 2 strands of floss.

Cross-Stitch Pictures   Shown on pages 24 and 25.

HOUSE
FABRIC: Beige Indian cloth (52 threads to 10cm), 23cm square.
THREADS: DMC 6-strand embroidery floss:
1/2 skein each of Golden Yellow (783), Pistachio Green (367),

Parakeet Green (904); small amount each of Raspberry Red (3688), Episcopal Purple (917), Plum (552), Moss Green (471), Forget-me-not Blue (813), Royal Blue (996) and Red Brown (918).

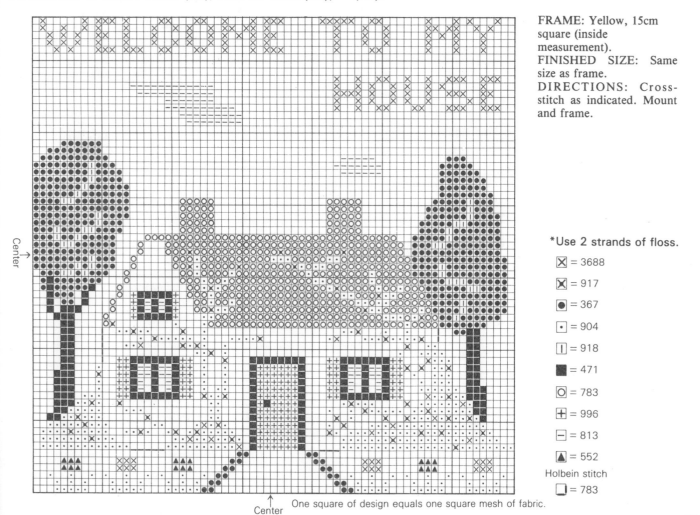

FRAME: Yellow, 15cm square (inside measurement).
FINISHED SIZE: Same size as frame.
DIRECTIONS: Cross-stitch as indicated. Mount and frame.

*Use 2 strands of floss.

⊠ = 3688

⊠ = 917

⬤ = 367

• = 904

▯ = 918

■ = 471

◯ = 783

✚ = 996

− = 813

▲ = 552

Holbein stitch
▯ = 783

Center

Center

One square of design equals one square mesh of fabric.

FLOWER BASKET

FABRIC: Beige Indian cloth (52 threads to 10cm), 23cm square.
THREADS: DMC 6-strand embroidery floss:
1/2 skein each of Raspberry Red (3688, 3685), Plum (552), Umber Gold (976), Moss Green (471), Parakeet Green (904); small amount each of Brilliant Green (704), Buttercup Yellow (444).

FRAME: Green, 15cm square (inside measurement).
FINISHED SIZE: Same size as frame.
DIRECTIONS: Cross-stitch as indicated. Mount and frame.

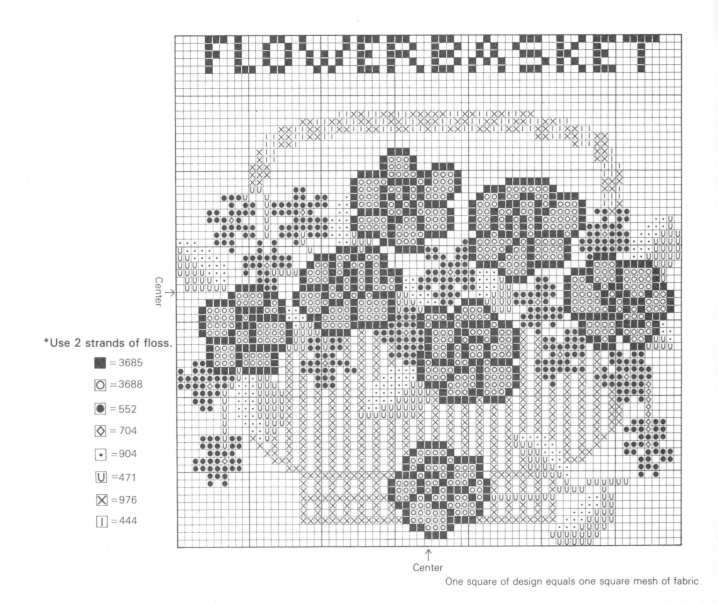

*Use 2 strands of floss.

■ = 3685
Ⓞ = 3688
● = 552
◈ = 704
• = 904
U = 471
☒ = 976
Ⅱ = 444

Center →

↑ Center

One square of design equals one square mesh of fabric.

How to prepare for Framing

1. Prepare a piece of carboard to fit frame.
2. Press wrong side of embroidered fabric, making sure that the grain is straight.
   Place cardboard on wrong side of fabric and fold back edges of fabric as shown.
3. With strong thread, stitch edges securely or use adhesive tape to secure fabric onto cardboard.

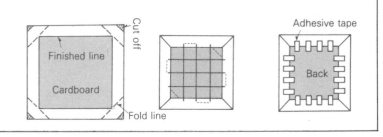

SAMPLER

FABRIC: Beige Java canvas (35 threads to 10cm), 37cm by 31cm.
THREADS: DMC 6-strand embroidery floss:
1-1/2 skeins of Brilliant Green (701): 1 skein of Forget-me-not Blue (826); 1/2 skein each of Cerise (604, 600), Brilliant Green (702), Laurel Green (988), Lemon Yellow (307), Poppy (666); small amount each of Geranium Red (754), Plum (552), Peacock Blue (807), Coffee Brown (938) and White.
FRAME: 29.3cm by 23.2cm (inside measurement).
FINISHED SIZE: Same size as frame.
DIRECTIONS: Cross-stitch as indicated. Mount and frame.

Center

Center

One square of design equals one square mesh of fabric.

Holbein stitch with 4 strands (666)

*Use 4 strands of floss.

⊙ = 826	✕ = 701	● = 666	△ = 307	I = White
• = 600	■ = 938	✛ = 988	◉ = 552	
V = 604	S = 754	⊗ = 702	✕ = 807	

57

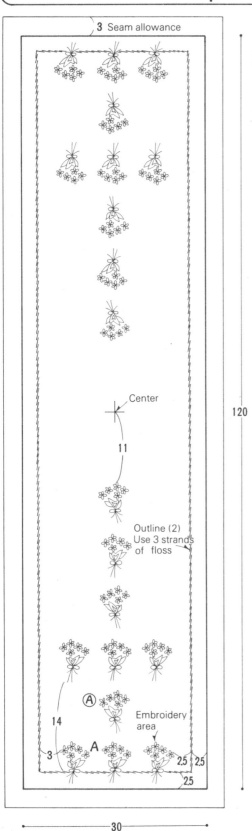

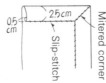

Detail of hem

3 Seam allowance

120

30

Center

11

Outline (2)
Use 3 strands
of floss

14

3

(A)

A

2.5   2.5

2.5

Embroidery
area

FABRIC: Unbleached Irish linen, 126cm by 36cm.
THREADS: Anchor 6-strand embroidery floss:
2 skeins of White (2); 1-1/2 skeins each of Soft Pink (48), Magenta Rose (23); 1 skein each of Soft Pink (73), Emerald Green (243), Brilliant Green (226); small amount of Canary Yellow (290).
FINISHED SIZE: 120cm by 30cm.
DIRECTIONS: Transfer design to fabric, reversing design for opposite side.
Embroider. Outline-stitch along hem. Finish with plain hem, mitering corners (see page 45).

Actual size
*Use 3 strands of floss unless otherwise indicated.
Reverse pattern A for (A).

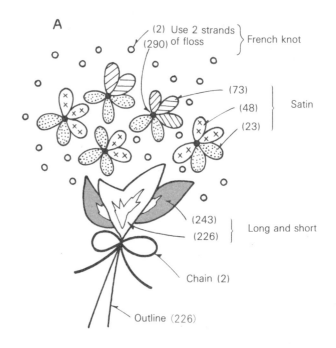

A

(2) Use 2 strands
(290) of floss } French knot

(73)
(48)   Satin
(23)

(243)
(226) } Long and short

Chain (2)

Outline (226)

Hop Aboard Cushions

Shown on pages 10 and 11.

MATERIALS FOR ONE CUSHION

FABRIC: Cream Java canvas (35 threads to 10cm), 91cm by 44cm.

THREADS: DMC 6-strand embroidery floss:

CAR-3 skeins of Royal Blue (796); 2 skeins of Flame Red (606); 1-1/2 skeins of Drab (610); 1 skein each of Brilliant Green (702), Forget-me-not Blue (828), Beaver Gray (645), Ash Gray (415), White, Black (310); 1/2 skein each of Mahogany (300), Smoke Gray (642) and Buttercup Yellow (444).

HELICOPTER-4 skeins of Beaver Gray (844); 2 skeins of Fire Red (900): 1 skein each of Emerald Green (910), Lemon Yellow (445); 1/2 skein each of Greenish Gray (598), Emerald Green (955), Forget-me-not Blue (828), Royal Blue (797), Tangerine Yellow (741), Beaver Gray (647) and Drab (610).

BUS-3 skeins of Emerald Green (954); 2-1/2 skeins of Flame Red (606); 2 skeins each of Forget-me-not Blue (828), Drab (610), Beaver Gray (844), White; 1 skein each of Buttercup Yellow (444), Royal Yellow (820); 1/2 skein each of Beaver Gray (645), Ash Gray (415) and Black (310).

NOTIONS: 35cm zipper. 43cm square inner pillow stuffed with kapok.

FINISHED SIZE: 40cm square.

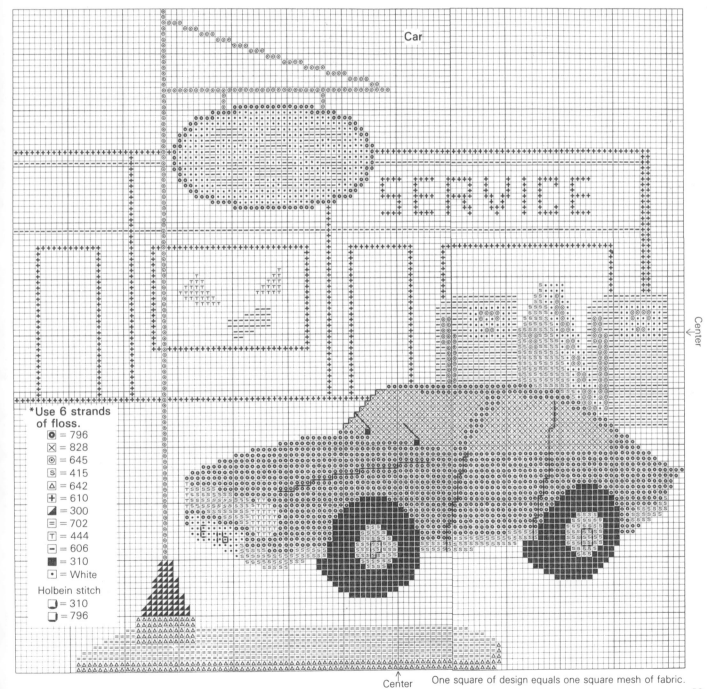

Car

Center

*Use 6 strands of floss.

- ⊙ = 796
- ✕ = 828
- ◎ = 645
- S = 415
- △ = 642
- ✚ = 610
- ◪ = 300
- ⊟ = 702
- T = 444
- ⊟ = 606
- ■ = 310
- ⊡ = White

Holbein stitch
- ▭ = 310
- ▭ = 796

Center

One square of design equals one square mesh of fabric.

DIRECTIONS: Cross-stitch as indicated. Sew zipper to back piece, sew front and back together with right sides facing, and turn inside out.
Insert inner pillow.

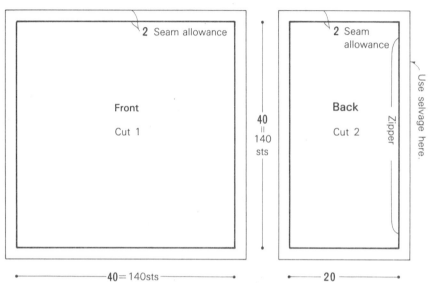

*Use 6 strands of floss.

Symbol	Color
●	= 844
◉	= 910
T	= 598
L	= 955
△	= 647
✚	= 610
◆	= 445
‖	= 741
U	= 900
X	= 828
◇	= 797

Holbein stitch

Symbol	Color
▭	= 844
▭	= 910

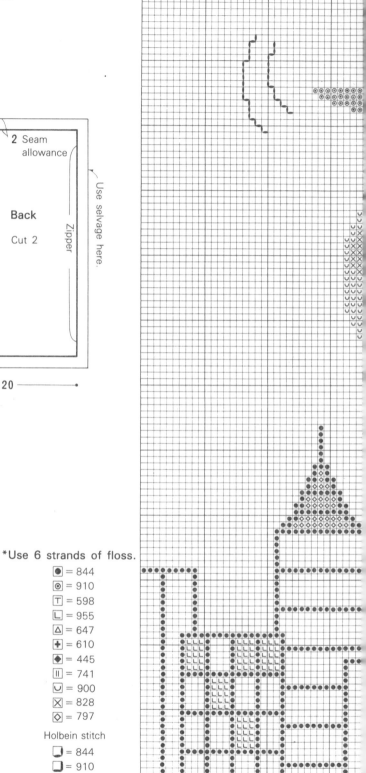

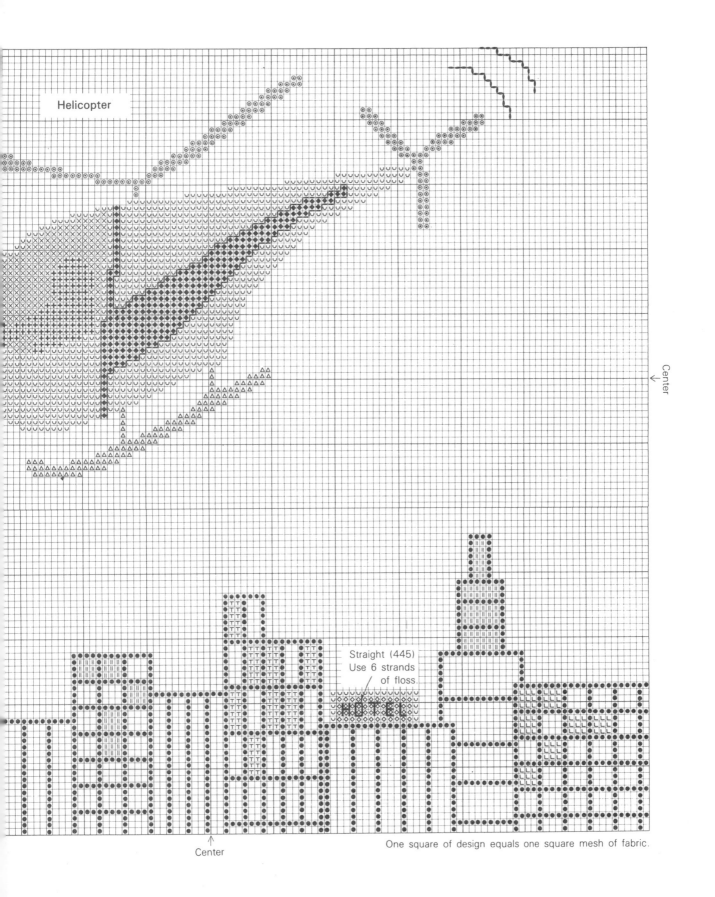

Helicopter

Straight (445)
Use 6 strands
of floss.

↓ Center

↑
Center

One square of design equals one square mesh of fabric.

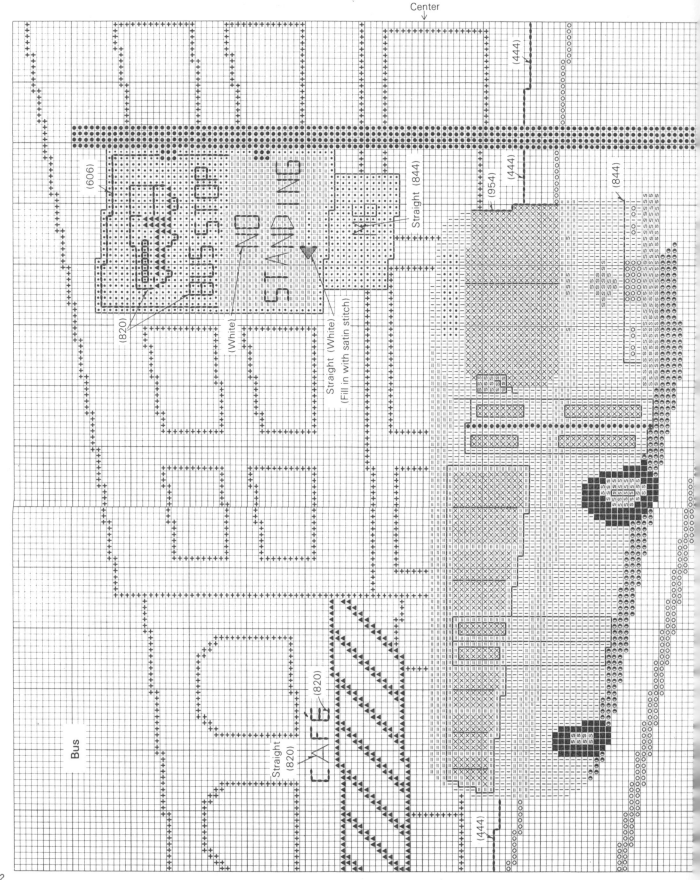

Center

(444)

(606)

Straight (844)

(954)

(444)

(844)

(White)

Straight (White)
(Fill in with satin stitch)

(820)

Bus

Straight
(820)

CAFE (820)

(444)

One square of design equals one square mesh of fabric.

↑ Center

Holbein stitch

□ = 844

□ □ = Use colors indicated.

• = White
■ = 310

○ = 444
∥ = 606
+ = 610

● = 844
S = 415
○ = 645

X = 828
◀ = 820
— = 954

*Use 6 strands of floss.

Country Scene Table Center
Shown on page 14.

FABRIC: Cream Indian cloth (52 threads to 10cm), 75cm by 47cm.
THREADS: DMC 6-strand embroidery floss:
1 skein each of Brilliant Green (704), Violet Mauve (327); 1/2 skein each of Scarab Green (3348, 3347), Parakeet Green (904), Moss Green (469), Sage Green (3013), Yellow Green (730), Pistachio Green (369), Myrtle Gray (926), Emerald Green (955, 913, 912), Umber (436); small amount each of Myrtle Gray (927), Brilliant Green (702), Scarlet (815), Raspberry Red (3685, 3687), Garnet Red (309, 326), Geranium Red (350, 351), Morocco Red (761), Tangerine Yellow (740), Smoke Gray (644, 640), Beige Brown (841, 842), Drab (610), Beige (3047), Umber Gold (977), Umber (433), Coffee Brown (938), Red Brown (920), Terra·Cotta (355), Saffron (725, 726), Copper Green (831), Cornflower Blue (793, 792, 791), Plum (550), Beaver Gray (645), Seagull Gray (452, 451), Sèvres Blue (800) and Antique Blue (932).
FINISHED SIZE: 68.5cm by 41cm.
DIRECTIONS: Cross-stitch as indicated, then stitch French knots and outline stitches as indicated. Finish with plain hem, mitering corners (see page 45).

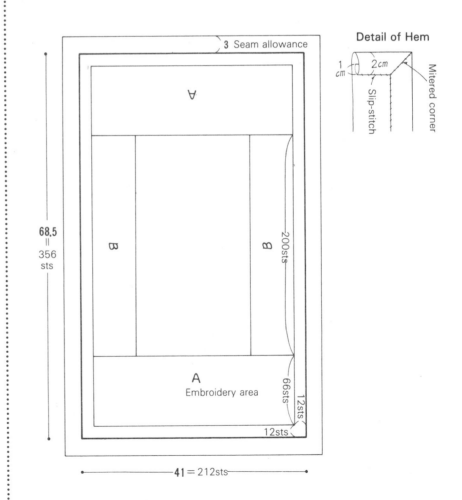

3 Seam allowance

Detail of Hem

1 cm   2cm

Slip-stitch   Mitered corner

A

B   B

68,5 = 356 sts

200sts

A
Embroidery area

66sts

12sts

12sts

41 = 212sts

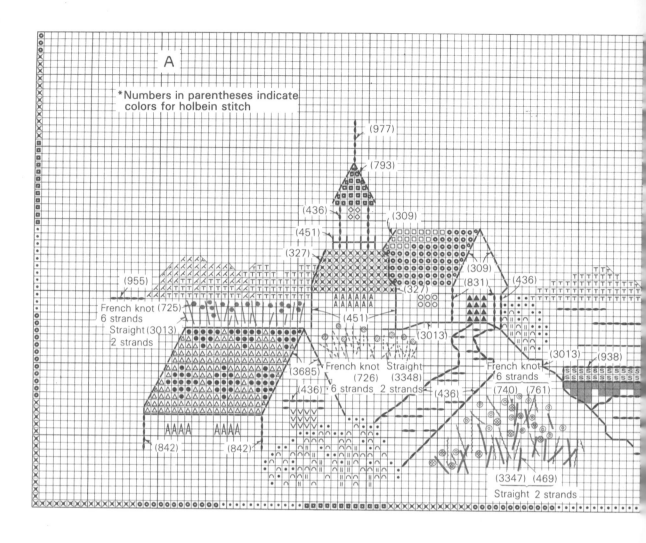

A

*Numbers in parentheses indicate colors for holbein stitch

(977)
(793)
(436)
(451)
(327)
(309)
(309)
(955)
(831)
(436)
French knot (725)
6 strands
Straight (3013)
2 strands
(451)
(3013)
(3013)
(938)
(3685)
French knot Straight
(726)   (3348)
(436)   6 strands 2 strands
(740) (761)
(436)
French knot
6 strands
(842)
(842)
(3347) (469)
Straight 2 strands

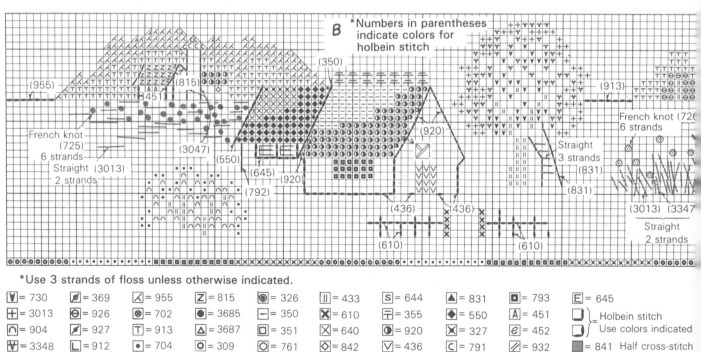

B *Numbers in parentheses indicate colors for holbein stitch

(350)
(955)
451
(815)
(913)
French knot (726)
6 strands
French knot
(725)
6 strands
(3047)
(920)
Straight
3 strands
Straight (3013)
2 strands
(550)
(831)
(645)
(920)
(831)
(792)
(436) (436)
(3013) (3347)
(610)
(610)
Straight
2 strands

*Use 3 strands of floss unless otherwise indicated.

▼ = 730	∅ = 369	⬈ = 955	Z = 815	◉ = 326
⊞ = 3013	⊖ = 926	⊗ = 702	● = 3685	– = 350
∩ = 904	✎ = 927	T = 913	△ = 3687	□ = 351
▼ = 3348	L = 912	• = 704	O = 309	O = 761

‖ = 433	S = 644	▲ = 831	▣ = 793	E = 645
X = 610	⊤ = 355	◆ = 550	A = 451	⬜ = Holbein stitch
X = 640	◑ = 920	X = 327	e = 452	⬜ = Use colors indicated
◇ = 842	V = 436	C = 791	⧄ = 932	▨ = 841 Half cross-stitch

64

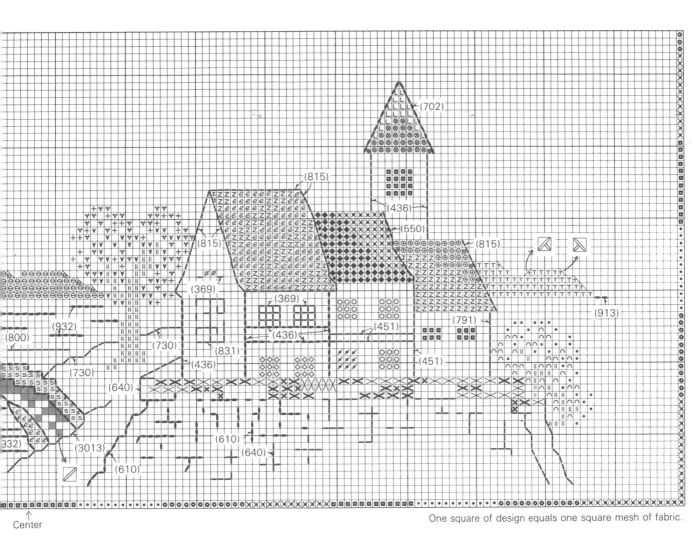

↑
Center

One square of design equals one square mesh of fabric.

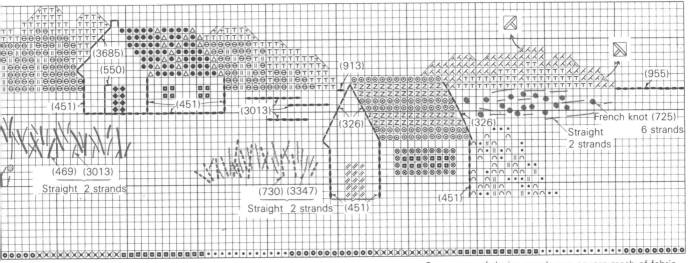

French knot (725)
Straight
2 strands
6 strands

(469) (3013)
Straight 2 strands

(730) (3347)
Straight 2 strands

One square of design equals one square mesh of fabric.

65

DAISIES, TOP
FABRIC: Olive Green Irish linen, 17cm square.
THREADS: DMC 6-strand embroidery floss:
small amount each of Green (3051), Pistachio Green (320), Laurel Green (988), Golden Yellow (783) and White.
FRAME: White, 9.2cm square (inside measurement). White mounting mat, same size as frame (inside measurement, 7.2cm square).
FINISHED SIZE: Same size as frame.
DIRECTIONS: Match centers of fabric and design, and transfer design to fabric. Embroider. Mount and frame.

Actual size   *Use 2 strands of floss.

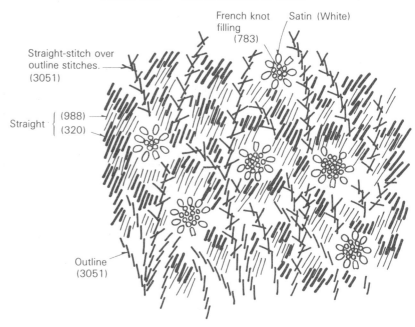

FIELD, BOTTOM
FABRIC: Mustard Irish linen, 17cm square.
THREADS: DMC 6-strand embroidery floss:
small amount each of Moss Green (471, 935), Scarab Green (3347), Pistachio Green (367), Drab (613, 610) and Geranium Pink (894).
FRAME: White, 9.2cm (inside measurement). White mounting mat, same size as frame (inside measurement, 7.2cm square).
FINISHED SIZE: Same size as frame.
DIRECTIONS: Match centers of fabric and design, and transfer design to fabric. Embroider. Mount and frame.

Actual size   *Use 2 strands of floss.

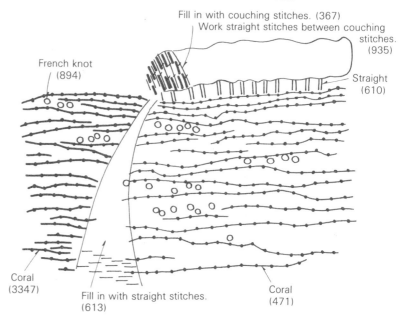

HOUSE AND TREE
FABRIC: Blue Irish linen, 25cm by 17cm.
THREADS: DMC 6-strand embroidery floss:
small amount each of Ivy Green (500), Scarab Green (3348), Green (3052), Pistachio Green (320), Emerald Green (913), Peacock Green (991), Geranium Red (350), Soft Pink (776), Beaver Gray (844), Drab (613, 610) and Ecru.

FRAME: White, 17cm by 9.2cm (inside measurement). White mounting mat, same size as frame (14cm by 7cm, inside measurement).
FINISHED SIZE: Same size as frame.
DIRECTIONS: Match centers of fabric and design, and transfer design to fabric.
Embroider. Mount and frame.

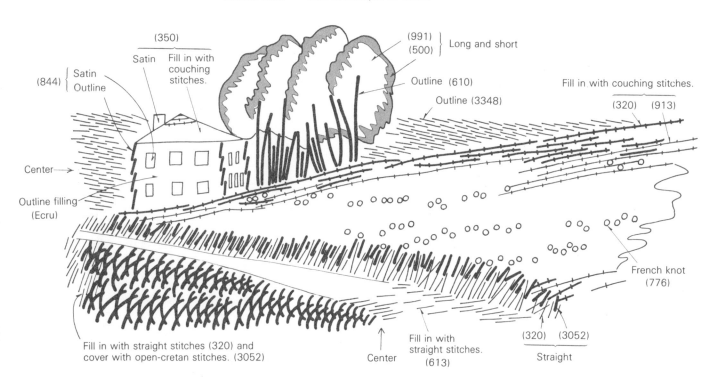

Actual size   *Use 2 strands of floss.

(350)
Satin   Fill in with couching stitches.
(844) { Satin
        Outline
Center →
Outline filling (Ecru)

(991)
(500) } Long and short
Outline (610)
Outline (3348)
Fill in with couching stitches.
(320)   (913)

French knot (776)

Fill in with straight stitches (320) and cover with open-cretan stitches. (3052)

Center

Fill in with straight stitches. (613)

(320)   (3052)
Straight

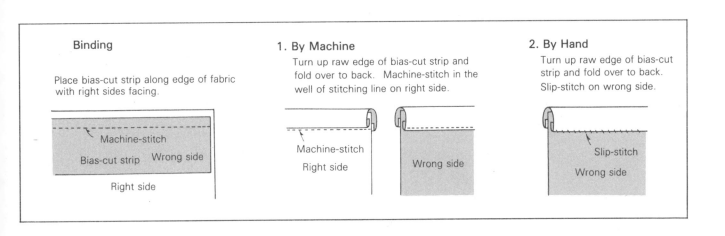

Binding

Place bias-cut strip along edge of fabric with right sides facing.

Machine-stitch
Bias-cut strip   Wrong side
Right side

1. By Machine

Turn up raw edge of bias-cut strip and fold over to back. Machine-stitch in the well of stitching line on right side.

Machine-stitch
Right side
Wrong side

2. By Hand

Turn up raw edge of bias-cut strip and fold over to back. Slip-stitch on wrong side.

Slip-stitch
Wrong side

Wall Hanging   Shown on page 27.

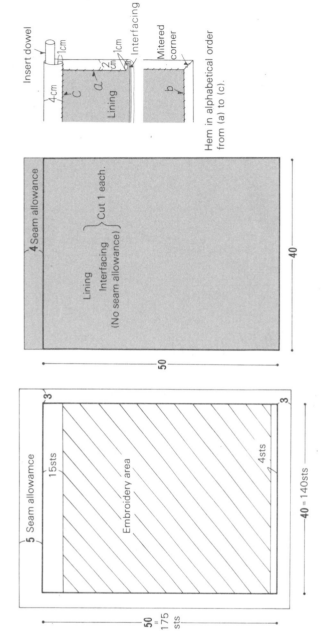

Insert dowel

Interfacing

1cm

4cm

c

a

2

1cm

Interfacing

Lining

Mitered corner

b

Hem in alphabetical order from (a) to (c).

4 Seam allowance

Lining

Interfacing
(No seam allowance)

Cut 1 each.

40

50

5 Seam allowance

15sts

Embroidery area

4sts

40 = 140sts

50 = 175 sts

3

3

FABRICS: Yellow-green Java canvas (35 threads to 10cm), 58cm by 46cm.
Heavy-weight cotton fabric for lining, 54cm by 40cm.

THREADS: DMC 6-strand embroidery floss:

2 skeins of Brilliant Green (701); 1-1/2 skeins of Soft Pink (776); 1 skein each of Brilliant Green (699), Forget-me-not Blue (824), Geranium Red (754), Coffee Brown (898), Raspberry Red (3685), Flame Red (608), Red Brown (918); 1/2 skein each of Forget-me-not Blue (827, 826), Royal Blue (797), Golden Yellow (782), Lemon Yellow (307), Emerald Green (911), Brilliant Green (703), Cerise (603); small amount each of Parakeet Green (904), Pistachio Green (319), Peacock Green (991), Sage Green (3012), Poppy (666), Plum (550), Saffron (726) and Black (310).

NOTIONS: Iron-on interfacing, 50cm by 40cm.

ACCESSORY: 1 dowel.

FINISHED SIZE: 50cm by 40cm.

DIRECTIONS: Cross-stitch as indicated. Press iron-on interfacing on wrong side of embroidered fabric. Hem as shown, mitering corners of bottom edge (see page 45).

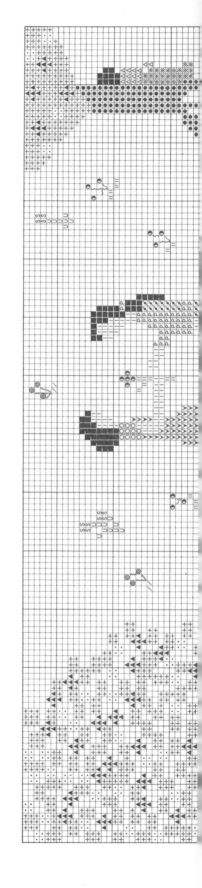

*Use 4 strands of floss.

Symbol	Color
+	= 701
·	= 776
U	= 699
▌	= 754
■	= 898
●	= 918
◀	= 3685
○	= 827
◉	= 826
◣	= 797
▨	= 824
▼	= 608
X	= 782
◁	= 307
✳	= 911
⁄	= 703
S	= 603
‖	= 904
T	= 319
P	= 991
◩	= 3012
◆	= 666
◐	= 550
◨	= 726
◣	= 310

Holbein stitch

Symbol	Color
⊡	= 898
⊡	= 904
▨	= 703
⊡	= 776

Wall Hanging with Pockets   Shown on page 28.

FABRIC: Irish linen, unbleached, 102cm by 59cm and Red, 148cm by 25cm.
THREADS: DMC 6-strand embroidery floss:
5-1/2 skeins of Ecru.
ACCESSORIES: One dowel, 1cm in diameter and 80cm long.
Cotton cord, 100cm long.
FINISHED SIZE: See diagram.

Actual size

A

Satin 3 strands

French knot

Outline filling { 4 strands

Outline

B

Satin 3 strands

Chain 3 strands

Outline filling

4 strands

French knot

4 strands

Straight

Outline

C

Chain
Satin
Outline

3 strands

Satin

French knot

Straight

4 strands

Outline filling

Fly

Outline

4 strands

D

Satin 3 strands

Fly

French knot

Coral

4 strands

Outline filling

Outline

Straight 3 strands

E

Chain

3 strands

Satin

French knot
4 strands

Satin
3 strands

Outline
3 strands

Straight

Outline filling

Couched trellis

4 strand.

Outline

70

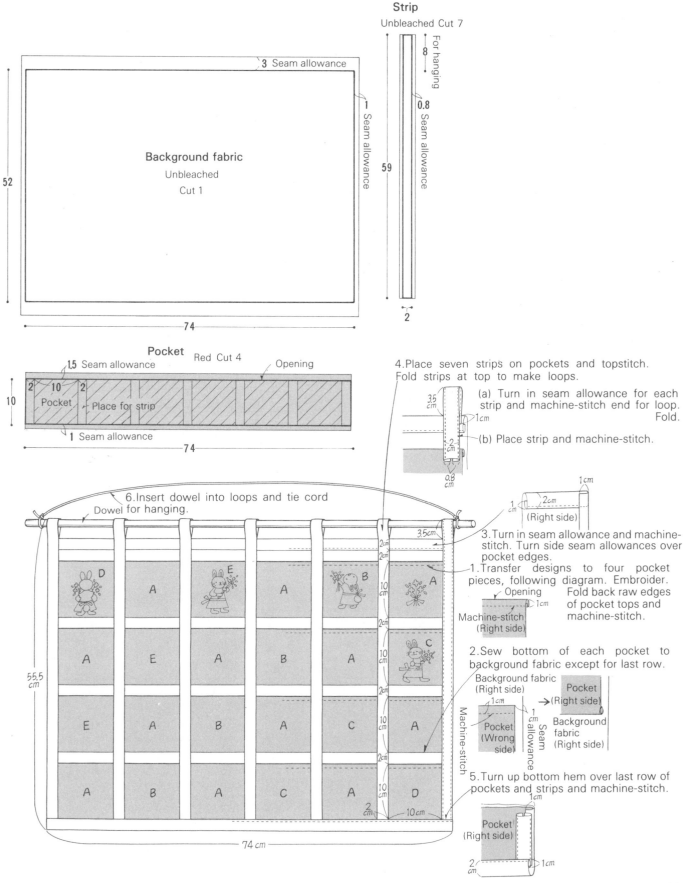

Strip

Unbleached Cut 7

For hanging

8

0.8 Seam allowance

59

2

3 Seam allowance

1 Seam allowance

Background fabric

Unbleached

Cut 1

52

74

Pocket Red Cut 4

1.5 Seam allowance

Opening

2 10 2

10 Pocket Place for strip

1 Seam allowance

74

4. Place seven strips on pockets and topstitch. Fold strips at top to make loops.

(a) Turn in seam allowance for each strip and machine-stitch end for loop. Fold.

(b) Place strip and machine-stitch.

3.5 cm

1cm

2 cm

0.8 cm

1cm

1 cm

2cm

(Right side)

3. Turn in seam allowance and machine-stitch. Turn side seam allowances over pocket edges.

1. Transfer designs to four pocket pieces, following diagram. Embroider. Fold back raw edges of pocket tops and machine-stitch.

Opening 1cm

Machine-stitch (Right side)

6. Insert dowel into loops and tie cord Dowel for hanging.

3.5cm

2cm
2cm

D   A   E   B   A

10 cm

2cm

A   E   A   B   A

10 cm

2cm

E   A   B   A   C   A

10 cm

2cm

A   B   A   C   A   D

10 cm

2 cm   10 cm

55.5 cm

Machine-stitch

Seam allowance

74 cm

2. Sew bottom of each pocket to background fabric except for last row.

Background fabric (Right side)

1cm

Pocket (Wrong side)

Pocket (Right side)

1 cm allowance

Background fabric (Right side)

5. Turn up bottom hem over last row of pockets and strips and machine-stitch.

1cm

Pocket (Right side)

2 cm   1cm

FABRIC: Pink Irish linen; 137cm by 116cm for Pillow Case, 110cm by 79cm for Border.

THREADS: Anchor 6-strand embroidery floss:

PILLOW CASE---1 skein each of White, Faded Pink (969); 1/2 skein each of Emerald Green (206), Green (843), Parma Violet (105,104), Violet Mauve (107), Peony Rose (24), Soft Pink (25), Morocco Red (76), Raspberry Red (78); small amount of Saffron (301).

BORDER FOR TOP SHEET---Use same color threads as Pillow Case.

NOTIONS: White lace edging (1.5cm wide), 280cm for Pillow Case and 245cm for Border. Velcro (2.5cm wide), 10cm.

FINISHED SIZE: Pillow Case, 80cm by 56cm (for 72cm by 48cm pillow). Border, 100cm by 70cm.

DIRECTIONS: FOR PILLOW CASE: Transfer design to fabric diagonally as shown in diagram. Embroider. Sew front and back pieces together with right sides facing. Turn inside out. Topstitch 4cm in from seam. Trim with lace edging. Sew velcro strip onto opening edge of back piece.

FOR BORDER: Transfer design to fabric horizontally as shown in diagram. Embroider. Hem as indicated. Trim three sides with lace edging.

Pillow Case

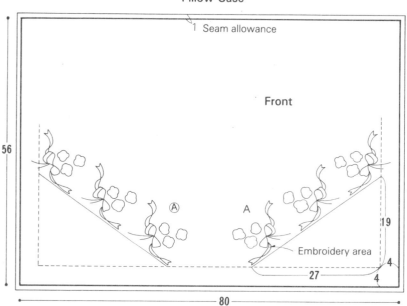

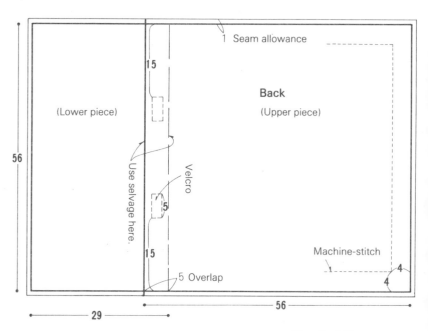

Detail of Hem

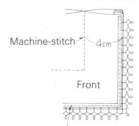

Place lace edging and machine-stitch.

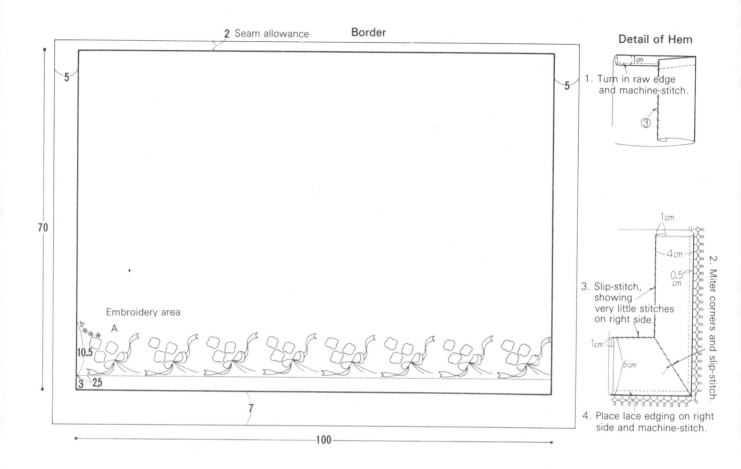

Border

2 Seam allowance

Detail of Hem

5

5

70

Embroidery area

A

10.5

3 25

7

100

1. Turn in raw edge and machine-stitch.

③

2. Miter corners and slip-stitch.

1cm

4cm

0.5 cm

3. Slip-stitch, showing very little stitches on right side.

1cm

6cm

4. Place lace edging on right side and machine-stitch.

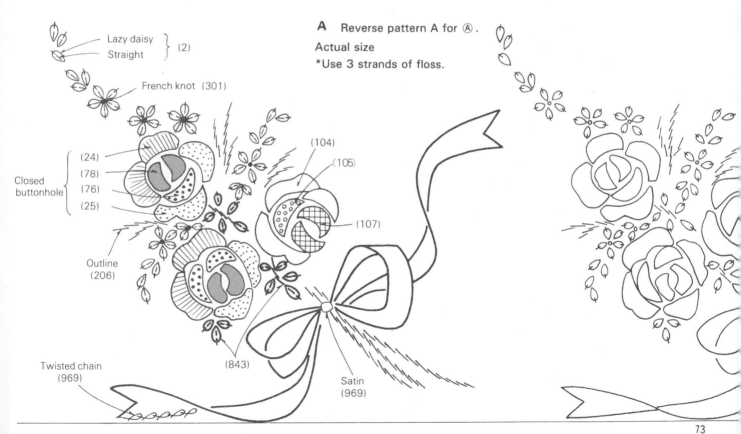

Lazy daisy
Straight } (2)

French knot (301)

A   Reverse pattern A for Ⓐ.

Actual size

*Use 3 strands of floss.

(24)
(78)
(76)
(25)

Closed buttonhole

(104)

(105)

(107)

Outline (206)

Twisted chain (969)

(843)

Satin (969)

Country House Table Center, Matching Curtain and Cushion

Shown on pages 18 and 19.

TABLE CENTER

FABRIC: Unbleached Irish linen, 94cm by 39cm.

THREADS: DMC 6-strand embroidery floss:

2-1/2 skeins of Laurel Green (988); 1-1/2 skeins of Almond Green (503); 1 skein each of Parakeet Green (904), Laurel Green (986); 1/2 skein of Geranium Red (350); small amount each of Golden Yellow (780), Smoke Gray (642), Mahogany (300), Hazelnut Brown (422) and Indigo (334).

FINISHED SIZE: 90cm by 35cm.

DIRECTIONS: Transfer design to fabric. Embroider. Finish with plain hem, mitering corners (see page 45).

Actual size   *Use 3 strands of floss unless otherwise indicated.

A

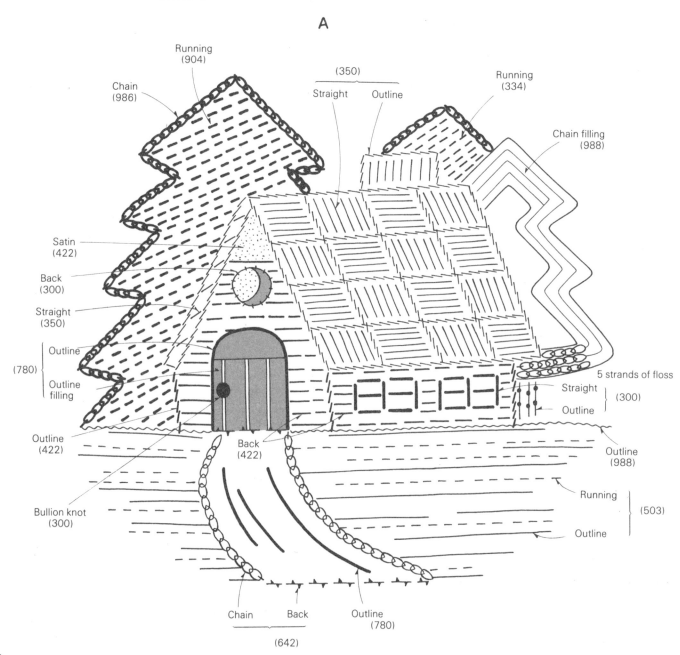

Detail of Hem

1cm

Slip-stitch

Mitered corner

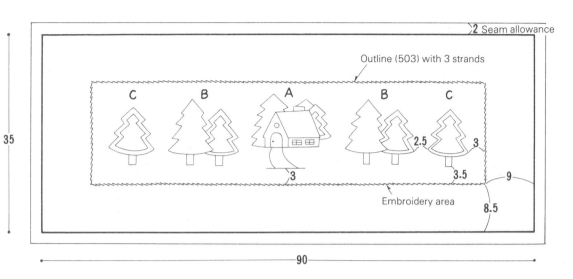

35

2 Seam allowance

Outline (503) with 3 strands

C   B   A   B   C

2.5   3

3   3.5

9

Embroidery area   8.5

90

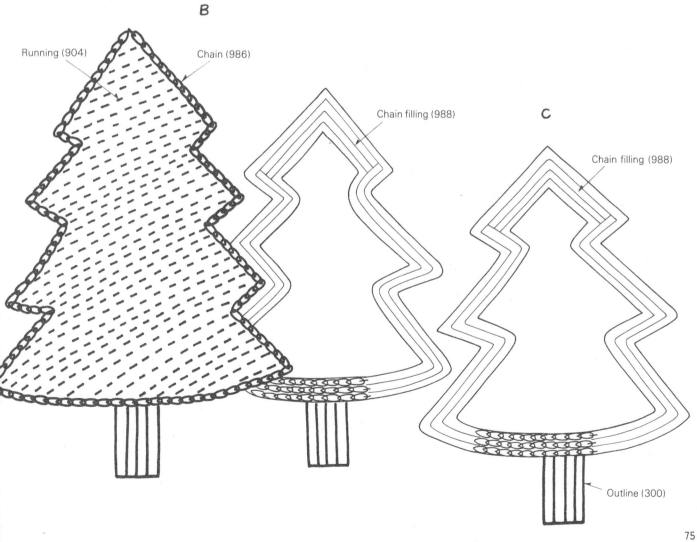

B

Running (904)   Chain (986)

Chain filling (988)   *C*

Chain filling (988)

Outline (300)

CURTAIN

FABRIC: Unbleached Irish linen, 98cm by 72cm.
THREADS: DMC 6-strand embroidery floss:
2-1/2 skeins of Laurel Green (988); 1-1/2 skeins each of Parakeet Green (904), Laurel Green (986); 1/2 skein of Geranium Red (350); small amount each of Almond Green(503), Golden Yellow (780), Smoke Gray (642), Mahogany (300), Hazelnut Brown (422) and Indigo (334).
FINISHED SIZE: 95cm by 60cm.
DIRECTIONS: Transfer design to fabric. Embroider. Finish hems as shown. Insert dowel into top hem.

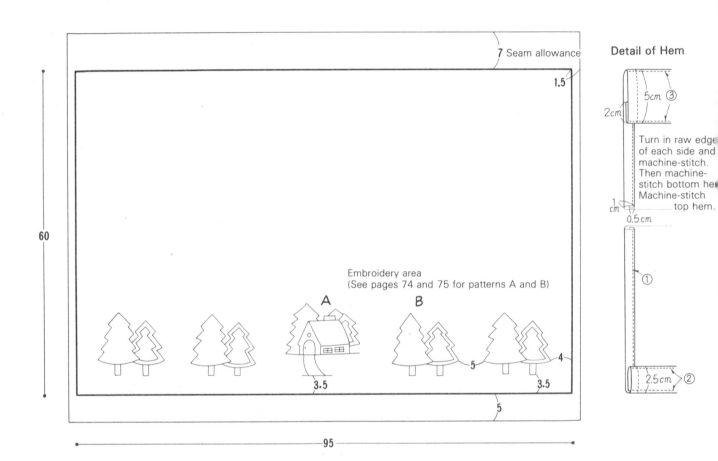

7 Seam allowance

Detail of Hem

1.5

5cm ③

2cm

Turn in raw edge of each side and machine-stitch. Then machine-stitch bottom hem. Machine-stitch top hem.

1 cm

0.5cm

60

Embroidery area
(See pages 74 and 75 for patterns A and B)

A   B

①

5   4

3.5   3.5

2.5cm ②

5

95

CUSHION

FABRIC: Irish linen, unbleached, 19cm square and Blue, 137cm by 43cm.
THREADS: DMC 6-strand embroidery floss:
1/2 skein of Geranium Red (350); small amount each of Laurel Green (988, 986), Parakeet Green (904), Almond Green (503), Golden Yellow (780), Smoke Gray (642), Mahogany (300), Hazelnut Brown (422) and Indigo (334).

DIRECTIONS: Transfer design to fabric. Embroider. Cut out 15cm square from center of front piece and clip corners. Tuck in seam allowance and place front piece on embroidered fabric, showing embroidery. Slip-stitch along folded edges. Sew zipper to back piece, sew front and back together with right sides facing, and turn inside out. Insert inner pillow.

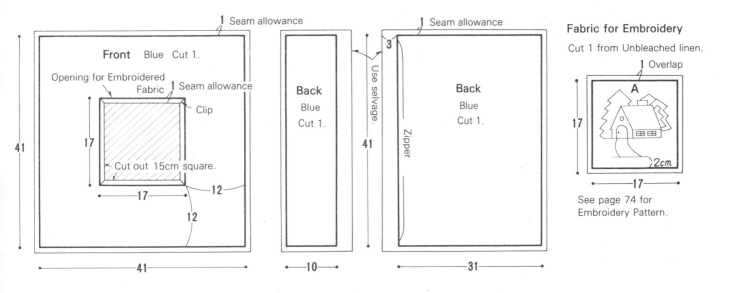

Front Blue Cut 1.

1 Seam allowance

Opening for Embroidered Fabric
1 Seam allowance

Clip

Cut out 15cm square.

41

17

17

12

12

Back Blue Cut 1.

1 Seam allowance

10

Use selvage.

41

3

1 Seam allowance

Back Blue Cut 1.

Zipper

31

Fabric for Embroidery

Cut 1 from Unbleached linen.

1 Overlap

A

17

2cm

17

See page 74 for Embroidery Pattern.

Personal Mug Placemats, Tray Mat   Shown on pages 18 and 19.

PLACEMAT

MATERIALS FOR ONE
FABRIC: Unbleached Irish linen, 43cm by 35cm.
THREADS: DMC 6-strand embroidery floss:
RIGHT---1 skein each of Morocco Red (760), Almond Green (504); 1/2 skein of Geranium Pink (891).
LEFT---1 skein each of Greenish Gray (598), Almond Green

(504); 1/2 skein of Royal Blue (796); small amount of Geranium Pink (891).
FINISHED SIZE: 40cm by 32cm.
DIRECTIONS: Transfer design to fabric. Embroider. Finish with plain hem. "Right" and "Left" in these instructions refer to the picture on pages 18 and 19.

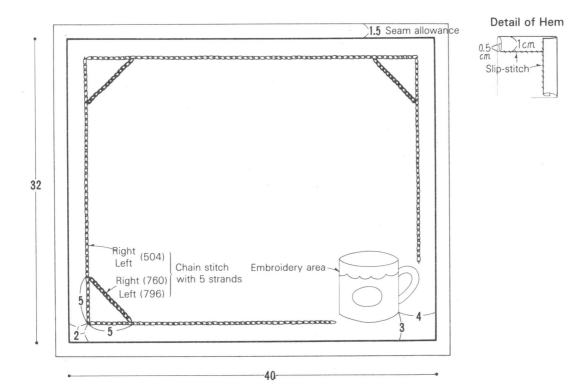

1.5 Seam allowance

Detail of Hem

0.5 cm
1cm
Slip-stitch

32

Right (504)
Left

Right (760)
Left (796)

Chain stitch with 5 strands

Embroidery area

5

5

2

3

4

40

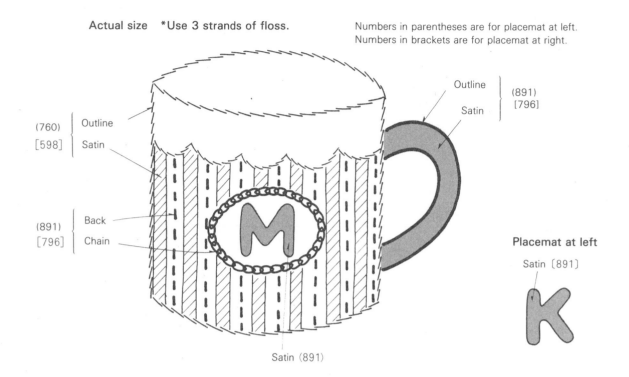

Actual size   *Use 3 strands of floss.

Numbers in parentheses are for placemat at left.
Numbers in brackets are for placemat at right.

Outline
Satin
(891)
[796]

(760) } Outline
[598] } Satin

(891) } Back
[796] } Chain

Satin (891)

Placemat at left

Satin [891]

TRAY MAT

FABRIC: Unbleached Irish linen, 41cm by 32cm.
THREADS: DMC 6-strand embroidery floss:
1 skein each of Morocco Red (760), Greenish Gray (598), Almond Green (504); 1/2 skein each of Geranium Pink (891), Royal Blue (796).

FINISHED SIZE: 38cm by 29cm.
DIRECTIONS: Transfer design to fabric. Embroider. Finish with plain hem.

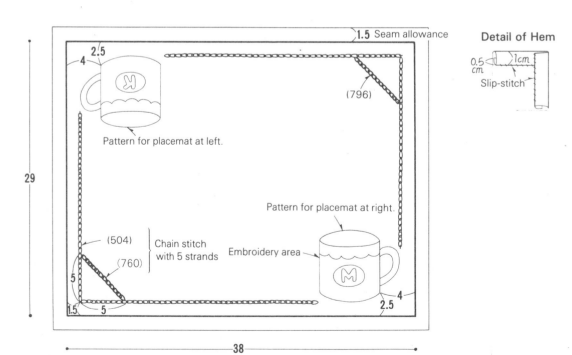

1.5 Seam allowance

2.5
4

(796)

Pattern for placemat at left.

29

(504)
(760)

Chain stitch
with 5 strands

Pattern for placemat at right.

Embroidery area

5

5
1.5   5

4
2.5

38

Detail of Hem

0.5 cm   1cm

Slip-stitch

Floral Bedspread   Shown on pages 30 and 31.

FABRICS: Beige Java canvas (35 threads to 10cm), 91cm by 540cm. Beige sheeting, 91cm by 498cm.

THREADS: DMC 6-strand embroidery floss:
6 skeins of Scarab Green (3348); 5 skeins of Coffee Brown (938); 4 skeins of Raspberry Red (3639); 3 skeins each of Laurel Green (988), Forget-me-not Blue (827, 809), White; 2-1/2 skeins of Saffron (727); 2 skeins each of Moss Green (472, 470), Scarab Green (3347), Laurel Green (986), Pistachio Green (368, 320), Brilliant Green (699), Raspberry Red (3688, 3685), Episcopal Purple (718), Soft Pink (819), Umber Gold (975), Cornflower Blue (794, 793, 792), Plum (554), Parma Violet (210, 208); 1 skein each of Moss Green (937, 936, 469), Pistachio Green (319), Garnet Red (326, 335), Geranium Pink (894, 893), Morocco Red (761), Ash Gray (415), Lemon Yellow (445), Umber Gold (977); 1/2 skein each of Moss Green (471), Indigo (939), Soft Pink (818), Cerise (600), Faded Pink (224), Morocco Red (760), Peony Rose (957), Old Rose (3350), Ash Gray (318), Buttercup Yellow (444), Light Yellow (3078), Saffron (725), Canary Yellow (972) and Umber Gold (976).

NOTIONS: Blue-gray grosgrain ribbon (2.6cm wide), 12.5cm.

FINISHED SIZE: 267cm by 170cm.

DIRECTIONS:
1. Match centers of fabric and design, and cross-stitch as indicated.
2. Join three embroidered pieces together with right sides facing. Place grosgrain ribbon on seam and slip-stitch.
3. Join pieces of lining fabric to make one piece 269cm by 166cm.
4. Sew embroidered piece and lining together with right sides faing, leaving top edge open. Turn inside out. Slip-stitch opening closed.
5. Place grosgrain ribbon along top and bottom edges and machine-stitch, then along each side and machine-stitch. Fold ends of ribbon to back.
6. Slip-stitch ends of ribbon.

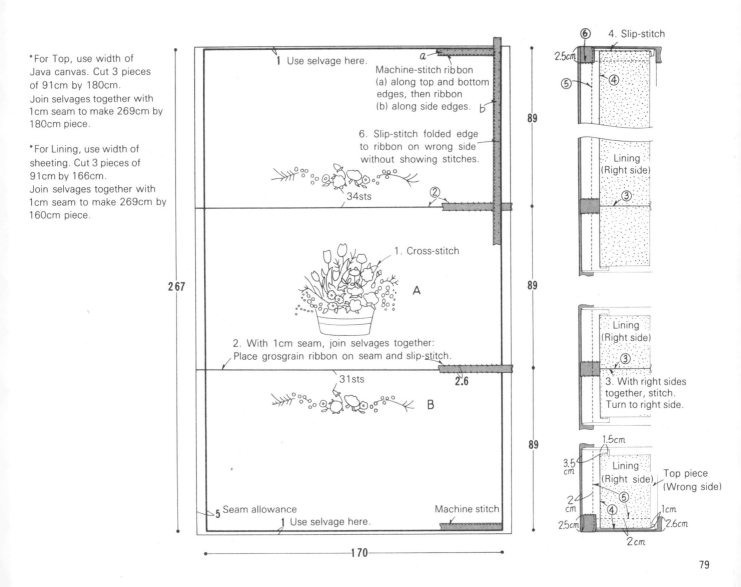

*For Top, use width of Java canvas. Cut 3 pieces of 91cm by 180cm.
Join selvages together with 1cm seam to make 269cm by 180cm piece.

*For Lining, use width of sheeting. Cut 3 pieces of 91cm by 166cm.
Join selvages together with 1cm seam to make 269cm by 160cm piece.

1 Use selvage here.

Machine-stitch ribbon (a) along top and bottom edges, then ribbon (b) along side edges.

6. Slip-stitch folded edge to ribbon on wrong side without showing stitches.

34sts

1. Cross-stitch

A

2. With 1cm seam, join selvages together. Place grosgrain ribbon on seam and slip-stitch.

31sts   2.6

B

Seam allowance

1 Use selvage here.

Machine stitch

267

170

89

89

89

4. Slip-stitch

2.5cm

Lining (Right side)

Lining (Right side)

3. With right sides together, stitch. Turn to right side.

1.5cm
3.5 cm
2.4 cm
2.5cm

Lining (Right side)   Top piece (Wrong side)

1cm
2.6cm
2 cm

79

Use 6 strands of floss.

◆ = 938   ▲ = 319
∩ = 3348   Φ = 937
○ = 988   ⊢ = 469
✳ = 827   ■ = 936
‖ = 809   ⊠ = 326
• = White   ⊗ = 335
△ = 472   ⊞ = 894
6 = 470   ◎ = 893
L = 3347   ╲ = 761
◇ = 986   ◪ = 415
A = 368   C = 445
◢ = 320   ◹ = 977
⊥ = 699   ⊠ = 471
⊞ = 3689   ■ = 939
U = 3688   V = 818
6 = 718   ▽ = 600
● = 3685   ▼ = 224
‖ = 819   ∅ = 760
Y = 727   ⊞ = 957
Z = 975   ◉ = 3350
< = 794   ◿ = 444
⊤ = 793   ℓ = 3078
◑ = 792   ✳ = 725
Y = 554   ▼ = 972
S = 208
⊟ = 210

Holbein stitch
  6 strands of floss
⊐ = 988
⊐ = 470
⊐ = 937
⊐ = 938
⊐ = 472
  3 strands of floss
⊐ = 600
⊐ = 318
⊐ = 976

80

Continued on next page.

A

Holbein stitch
(976)
with 3
strands

Center

One square of design equals one square mesh of fabric.

enter

Continued from Chart B.

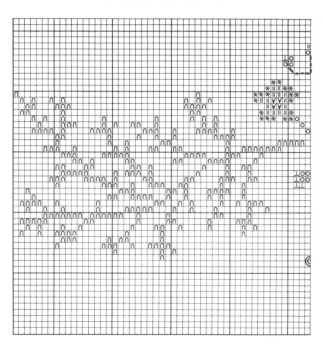

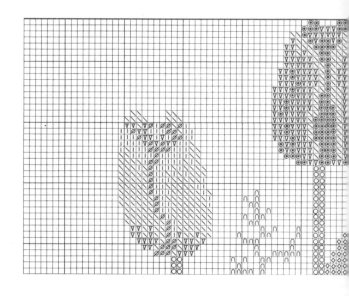

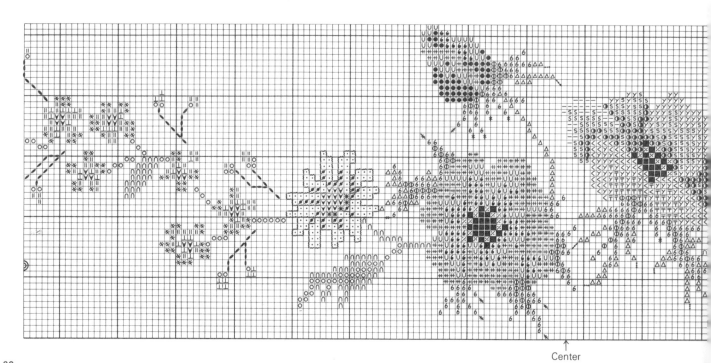

Center

Continued from Chart A.

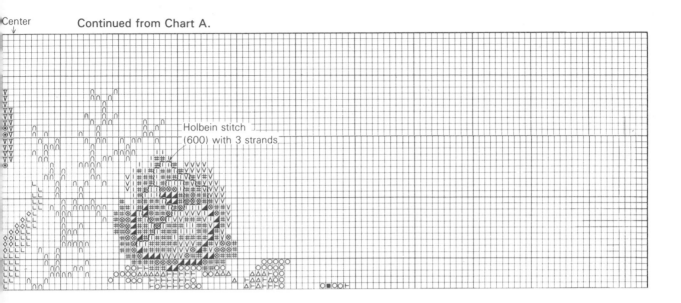

Holbein stitch
(600) with 3 strands

B

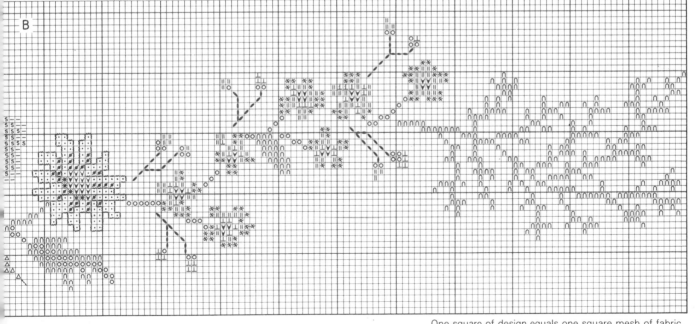

One square of design equals one square mesh of fabric.

Patchwork Tea Cozy and Toaster Cover Shown on page 36.

TEA COZY
FABRICS: Cotton fabric: Beige, Pistachio Green, Cream, Blue, Pink, 91cm by 14cm each. Beige sheeting for lining, 84cm by 36cm.
THREADS: DMC 6-strand embroidery floss:
1/2 skein each of Indigo (823), Umber (435); small amount each of Emerald Green (912), Brilliant Green (699), Drab (612), Sèvres Blue (798), Cerise (602), Flame Red (606), Tangerine Yellow (743), Geranium Red (351).
NOTIONS: Quilt batting, 80cm by 34cm.
FINISHED SIZE: 40cm wide and 34cm deep.
DIRECTIONS: Cut fabric. Join patches together following diagram. Transfer design to patched piece and embroider. Sew front and back pieces together with right sides facing, leaving bottom open. Cut off excess around curve. Turn inside out. Sew front and back pieces of lining with right sides facing. Insert lining into top piece, place quilt batting between two layers, and fix three layers with several stitches. Turn in bottom edges and slip-stitch.

Actual size

*Use 2 strands of floss.

——— Back stitch (823)

Make one piece each for Front and Back.

Top piece---Patchwork letters in brackets
indicate colors for Back piece
Lining---Sheeting
Quilt batting No seam allowance

Add 1cm seam allowance

Add 1cm seam allowance and cut out.

Fill in with Couching stitch (612)

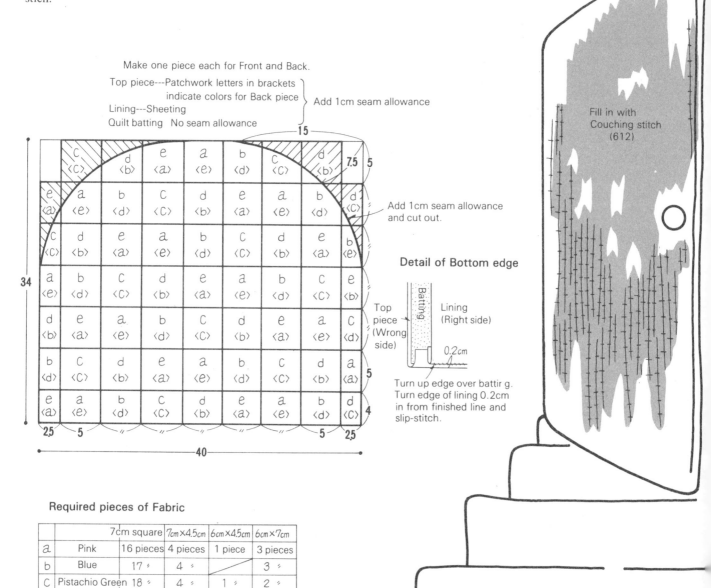

Detail of Bottom edge

Top piece (Wrong side) Batting Lining (Right side)

0.2cm

Turn up edge over batting.
Turn edge of lining 0.2cm in from finished line and slip-stitch.

Required pieces of Fabric

		7cm square	7cm×4.5cm	6cm×4.5cm	6cm×7cm
a	Pink	16 pieces	4 pieces	1 piece	3 pieces
b	Blue	17 ″	4 ″		3 ″
C	Pistachio Green	18 ″	4 ″	1 ″	2 ″
d	Cream	17 ″	4 ″	1 ″	3 ″
e	Beige	16 ″	4 ″	1 ″	3 ″

Come in.

Hi

Back   French knot   Chain
(823)

Satin
(435)

Fill in with Straight (351)

POST

Satin
(912)   (699)   (602)

← Center

Satin (606)

Satin (743)

Satin
Outline } (798)

↑
Center

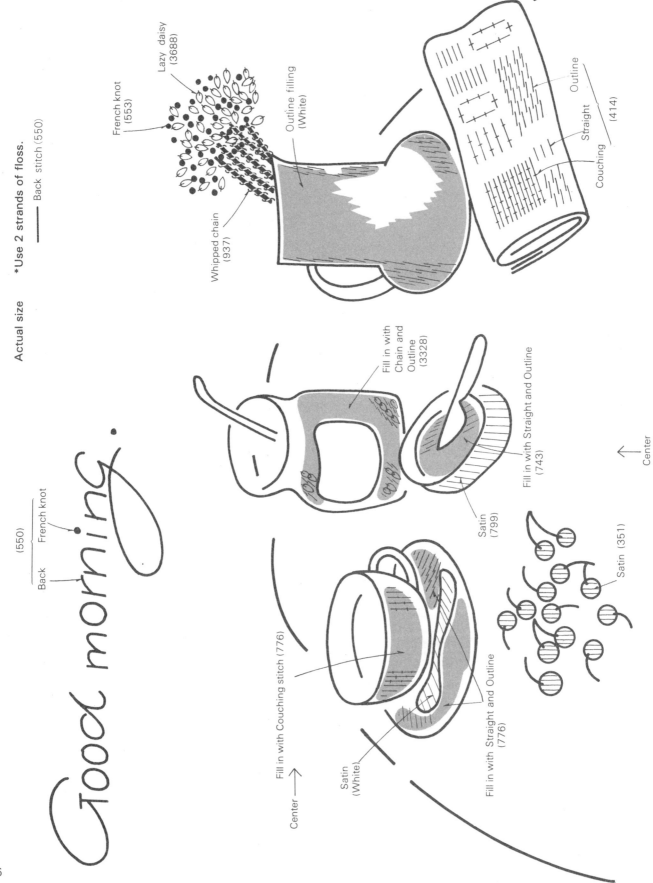

Actual size

*Use 2 strands of floss.
—— Back stitch (550)

French knot (553)

Lazy daisy (3688)

Outline filling (White)

Whipped chain (937)

Outline (414)

Straight

Couching

Fill in with Chain and Outline (3328)

Fill in with Straight and Outline (743)

Satin (799)

Satin (351)

Center

Fill in with Couching stitch (776)

Satin (White)

Fill in with Straight and Outline (776)

Center

Good morning.

(550)
French knot

Back

86

TOASTER COVER

FABRICS: Cotton fabric: Blue, 91cm by 21cm and Pistachio Green, Cream, Pink, 70cm by 7cm each and Beige, 14cm square. Beige sheeting for lining, 66cm by 39cm.
THREADS: DMC 6-strand embroidery floss:
small amount each of Ash Gray (414), Sèvres Blue (799), Tangerine Yellow (743), Geranium Red (351), Soft Pink (776), Morocco Red (3328), Plum (553, 550), Raspberry Red (3688), Moss Green (937) and White.

FINISHED SIZE: See diagram.
DIRECTIONS: Cut fabric. Join patches together following diagram. Transfer design to patched piece and embroider. Sew front, gusset and back pieces together with right sides facing. Turn inside out. Sew pieces for lining in same manner. Insert lining into top piece. Turn in bottom edges and slip-stitch.

Front and Back   Cut 1 each   *Add 1cm seam allowance.

Top piece---Patchwork
Lining---Sheeting

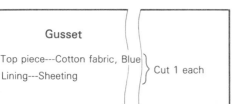

Required pieces of Fabric

		7cm square	6.5cm×7cm
a	Pink	6 pieces	4 pieces
b	Blue	6 ⸗	2 ⸗
c	Pistachio Green	8 ⸗	2 ⸗
d	Cream	6 ⸗	2 ⸗
e	Beige	4 ⸗	

Gusset

Top piece---Cotton fabric, Blue
Lining---Sheeting
} Cut 1 each

Detail of Bottom edge

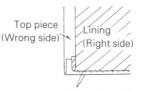

Top piece (Wrong side)
Lining (Right side)

Turn in raw edge of lining, 0.2cm in from finished line and slip-stitch.

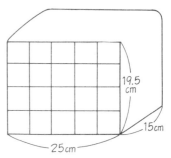

Flower Garden Picture   Shown on page 26.

FABRIC: Dark Beige Irish linen, 50cm by 37cm.
THREADS: Anchor 6-strand embroidery floss:
1-1/2 skeins of Beige Brown (936), 1 skein each of Almond Green (209), Moss Green (266), Geranium Red (52), Soft Pink (26); 1/2 skein each of Brilliant Green (225, 226, 227), Parma Violet (108, 110), Beige Brown (378), Canary Yellow (302), Azure Blue (160), Seagull Gray (399), Soft Pink (25); small amount each of Peony Rose (54), Cornflower Blue (117), Parma Violet (109) and Emerald Green (243).
FRAME: 20cm by 33.5cm (inside measurement).
FINISHED SIZE: Same size as frame.
DIRECTIONS: Transfer design to fabric. Embroider. Mount and frame.

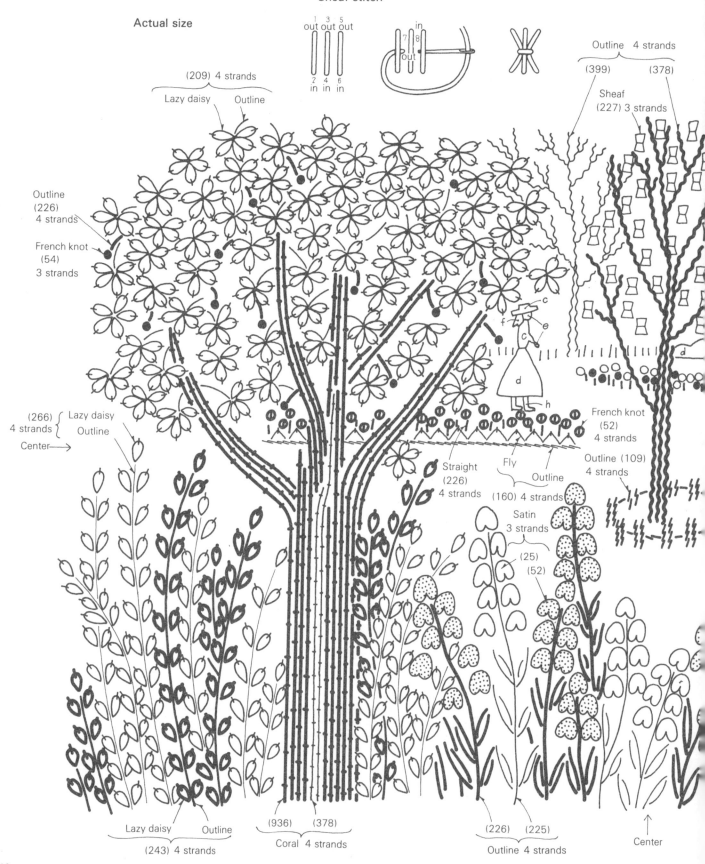

Sheaf stitch

Actual size

1 3 5
out out out
2 4 6
in in in

in
7 8
out
in

(209) 4 strands

Lazy daisy   Outline

Outline   4 strands
(399)   (378)

Sheaf
(227) 3 strands

Outline
(226)
4 strands

French knot
(54)
3 strands

(266) { Lazy daisy
4 strands { Outline

Center →

c
f   e
c
d

h

Straight
(226)
4 strands

Fly
Outline
(160) 4 strands

d

French knot
(52)
4 strands

Outline (109)
4 strands

Satin
3 strands

(25)
(52)

Lazy daisy   Outline

(243) 4 strands

(936)   (378)

Coral 4 strands

(226)   (225)

Outline 4 strands

Center

88

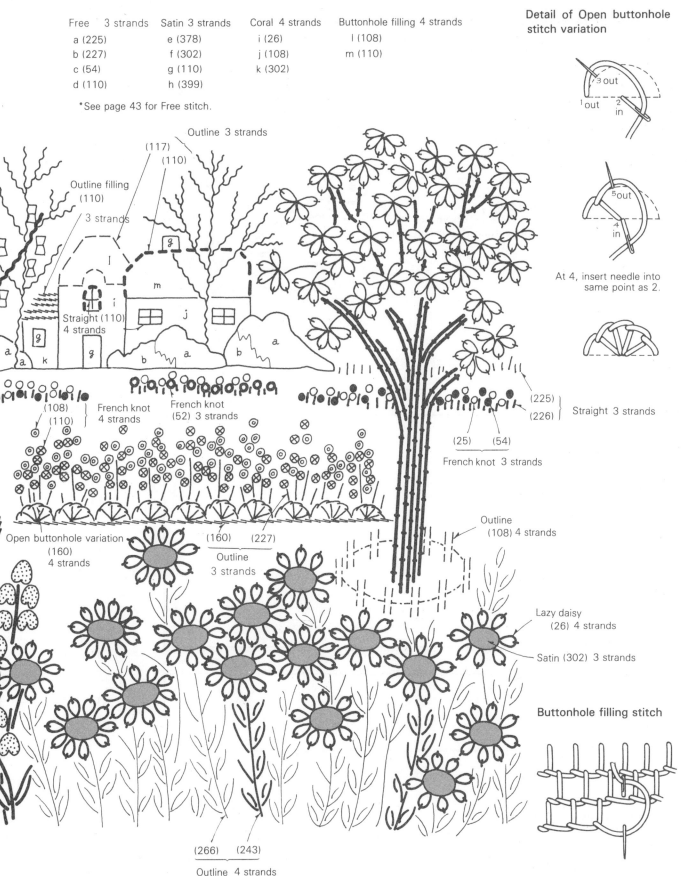

Free   3 strands
a (225)
b (227)
c (54)
d (110)

Satin 3 strands
e (378)
f (302)
g (110)
h (399)

Coral 4 strands
i (26)
j (108)
k (302)

Buttonhole filling 4 strands
l (108)
m (110)

*See page 43 for Free stitch.

Outline 3 strands
(117)
(110)

Outline filling
(110)

3 strands

Straight (110)
4 strands

French knot
(108)
(110)

French knot
4 strands

French knot
(52) 3 strands

(225)
(226) Straight 3 strands

(25)   (54)
French knot 3 strands

Outline
(108) 4 strands

Open buttonhole variation
(160)
4 strands

(160)   (227)
Outline
3 strands

Lazy daisy
(26) 4 strands

Satin (302) 3 strands

(266)   (243)
Outline 4 strands

Detail of Open buttonhole stitch variation

3 out
1 out   2 in

5 out
4 in

At 4, insert needle into same point as 2.

Buttonhole filling stitch

Lace-insert Curtain, Cushions, Tablecloth and Napkins

Shown on pages 16 and 17.

CURTAIN

MATERIALS FOR ONE PIECE

FABRIC: Unbleached Irish linen, 99cm by 67cm.

THREADS: DMC 6-strand embroidery floss:
1-1/2 skeins each of Turkey Red (321), Green (3051); 1 skein of Peacock Green (991).

NOTIONS: White ladder lace (0.8cm wide), 100cm. White cotton lace edging (4cm wide), 100cm.

FINISHED SIZE: 95cm by 63.5cm.

DIRECTIONS: Cut fabric. Transfer design to fabric and embroider. Sew curtain following numbered directions.

Actual size   *Use 3 strands of floss unless otherwise indicated.

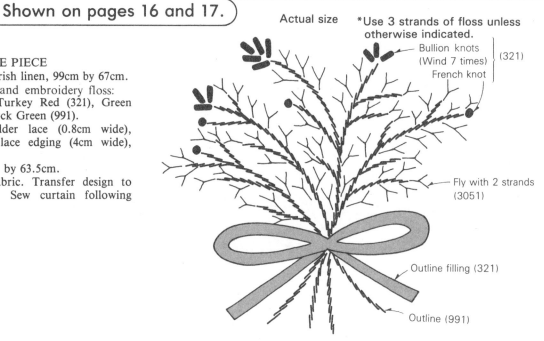

Bullion knots (Wind 7 times) (321)

French knot

Fly with 2 strands (3051)

Outline filling (321)

Outline (991)

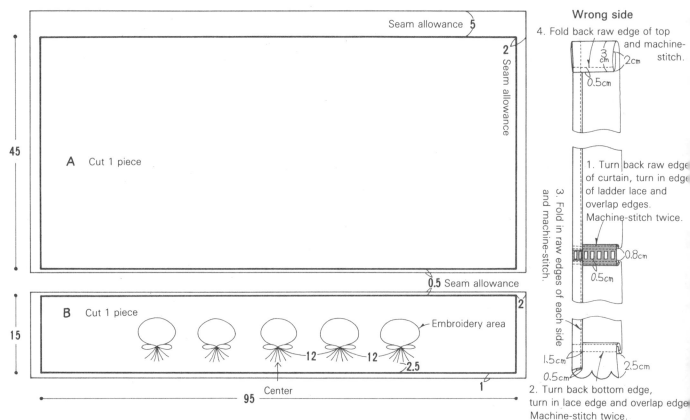

Seam allowance 5

2

Seam allowance

A Cut 1 piece

45

0.5 Seam allowance

2

B Cut 1 piece

Embroidery area

15

12   12

2.5

Center

95

1

Wrong side

4. Fold back raw edge of top and machine-stitch.

3cm   2cm

0.5cm

1. Turn back raw edge of curtain, turn in edge of ladder lace and overlap edges. Machine-stitch twice.

0.8cm

0.5cm

3. Fold in raw edges of each side and machine-stitch.

1.5cm   2.5cm

0.5cm

2. Turn back bottom edge, turn in lace edge and overlap edges. Machine-stitch twice.

PILLOW, SHOWN AT BOTTOM

FABRIC: Unbleached Irish linen, 98cm by 47cm.

THREADS: DMC 6-strand embroidery floss:
1/2 skein each of Turkey Red (321), Green (3051), Peacock Green (991).

NOTIONS: White ladder lace (0.8cm wide), 124cm. White cotton lace edging (4cm wide), 280cm. 40cm zipper. 47cm square inner pillow stuffed with kapok.

FINISHED SIZE: 45cm square.

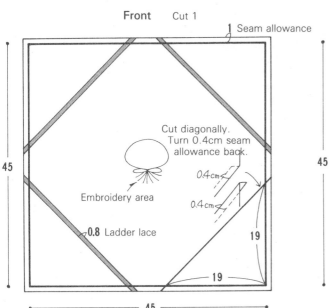

Front   Cut 1

Seam allowance

Cut diagonally.
Turn 0.4cm seam
allowance back.

Embroidery area

0.4cm

0.4cm

0.8 Ladder lace

45

45

19

19

*See page 90 for embroidery pattern and how to sew ladder lace.

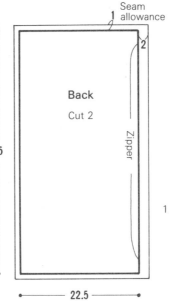

Seam allowance

Back

Cut 2

45

Zipper

22.5

DIRECTIONS: Cut off triangles from corners, and sew center piece and triangles with ladder lace inserted. Transfer design to center and embroider.
Sew zipper to back piece. Sew cushion following numbered directions. Insert inner pillow.

1. Gather lace.

3. Zigzag-stitch along raw edges.

1cm

3cm

2. With right sides of front and back pieces together and lace in between, stitch all around.

CUSHION, SHOWN AT TOP

FABRIC: Unbleached Irish linen, 137cm by 71cm.
THREADS: DMC 6-strand embroidery floss:
1/2 skein each of Turkey Red (321), Green (3051), Peacock Green (991).
NOTIONS: White ladder lace (0.8cm wide), 100cm. Cotton cord (0.2cm in diameter), 185cm; 40cm zipper; 47cm square inner pillow stuffed with kapok.
FINISHED SIZE: 45cm square.
DIRECTIONS: Cut fabric. Make corded piping following diagram. Sew four pieces of front together with ladder lace inserted. Transfer design to joined piece and embroider. Sew zipper

to back piece, and sew front and back pieces together with right sides facing and corded piping in between. Turn inside out. Insert inner pillow.

Actual size
*Use 3 strands of floss unless otherwise indicated.

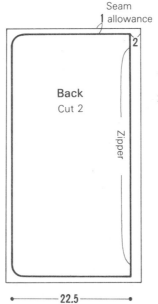

Bullion stitch
(Wind 7 times) (321)
French knot

Fly (3051) with 2 strands

Outline (991)

Front
Cut 4 pieces 23.5cm square.

Seam allowance

0.8

0.5cm
seam allowance

a

4

4

a

Embroidery area

0.8 Sew ladder lace
(a) first, then lace (b),
in same manner as
for Curtain.

45

22

22

b

45

Seam allowance

Back

Cut 2

45

Zipper

22.5

To Make Corded Piping

1. Join bias tape, 2.8cm wide, to make 185cm strip.
2. Fold in half lengthwise, place cotton cord between tape and machine-stitch.

0.4cm

1cm

Joining

1cm

With right sides of front and back pieces together and corded piping in between, stitch all around.

TABLECLOTH

FABRIC: Unbleached Irish linen, 137cm by 360cm.
THREADS: DMC 6-strand embroidery floss:
1-1/2 skeins each of Turkey Red (321), Green (3051); 1 skein of Peacock Green (991).
NOTIONS: White ladder lace (0.8cm wide), 710cm. White cotton lace edging (4cm wide), 710cm.
FINISHED SIZE: 209.5cm by 137.5cm.
DIRECTIONS: Cut fabric. Transfer design to fabric and embroider. Sew pieces together with ladder lace inserted. Fold back raw edges and trim with lace edging.

*Add 0.5cm seam allowance to edges to be joined with ladder lace.

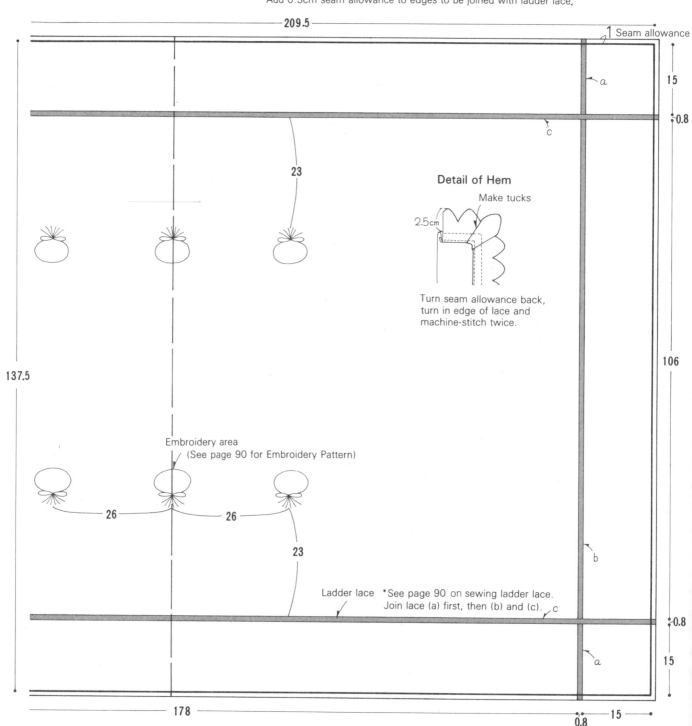

Detail of Hem

Make tucks

2.5cm

Turn seam allowance back, turn in edge of lace and machine-stitch twice.

Embroidery area
(See page 90 for Embroidery Pattern)

Ladder lace   *See page 90 on sewing ladder lace.
Join lace (a) first, then (b) and (c).

Seam allowance

NAPKIN
MATERIALS FOR ONE
FABRIC: Unbleached Irish linen, 39cm square.
THREADS: DMC 6-strand embroidery floss:
small amount each of Turkey Red (321), Green (3051), Peacock Green (991).

NOTIONS: White ladder lace (0.8cm wide), 30cm.
FINISHED SIZE: 36cm square.
DIRECTIONS: Cut fabric. Sew pieces A and B, inserting ladder lace in between. Transfer design to fabric and embroider. Finish with plain hem by machine-stitch.

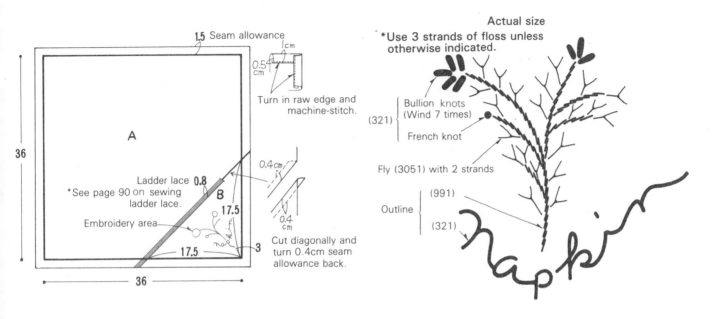

Actual size
*Use 3 strands of floss unless otherwise indicated.

Bullion knots (Wind 7 times) (321)
French knot
Fly (3051) with 2 strands
Outline { (991) (321) }

1.5 Seam allowance
1cm
0.5 cm
Turn in raw edge and machine-stitch.

A

36

Ladder lace 0.8
*See page 90 on sewing ladder lace.
B
Embroidery area
17.5
17.5
3
36

0.4cm
0.4 cm
Cut diagonally and turn 0.4cm seam allowance back.

Vegetable Placemats   Shown on age 37.

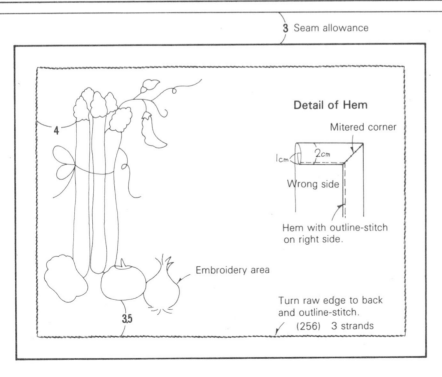

3 Seam allowance

29

4

Embroidery area

3.5

39

Detail of Hem
Mitered corner
1cm
2cm
Wrong side
Hem with outline-stitch on right side.
Turn raw edge to back and outline-stitch.
(256)   3 strands

MATERIALS FOR ONE
FABRIC: Cream Irish linen, 45cm by 35cm.
THREADS: Anchor 6-strand embroidery floss:
1 skein of Laurel Green (256); small amount each of Scarab Green (254), Parakeet Green (257), Laurel Green (258), Brilliant Green (225, 226, 227, 228), Canary Yellow (302), Tangerine Yellow (303), Umber Gold (347, 349) and Flame Red (335).
FINISHED SIZE: 39cm by 29cm.
DIRECTIONS: Transfer design to fabric and embroider. Fold back raw edges and outline-stitch on right side, stitching through folded edges and mitering corners (see page 45).

Actual size
*Use 3 strands of floss. Work in outline stitch unless otherwise indicated.

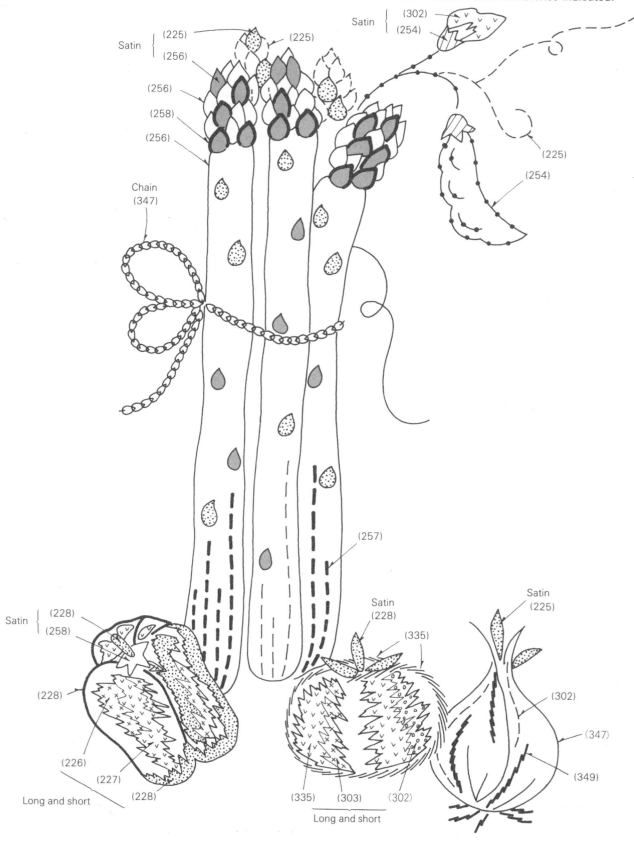

Coasters   Shown on page 37.

FABRIC (MATERIALS FOR ONE): Cream Irish linen, 12cm square.

THREADS: DMC 6-strand embroidery floss:
ORANGE COASTER---small amount each of Laurel Green (988), Canary Yellow (972), Tangerine Yellow (742), Umber Gold (976), Umber (738) and Hazelnut Brown (422). BROWN COASTER---small amount each of Scarab Green (3347), Umber Gold (977), Indian Red (3042), Raspberry Red (3687) and Scarlet (902). YELLOW GREEN COASTER---small amount each of Scarab Green (3347), Canary Yellow (972, 971), Umber (738), Hazelnut Brown (422), Beige Brown (841), Geranium Red (351) and White.

NOTIONS: Bias tape; Orange, Brown, Yellow-green (1.2cm wide), 40cm each.

FINISHED SIZE: 11.5cm in diameter.

DIRECTIONS: Transfer design to fabric and embroider. Sew Coaster as shown.

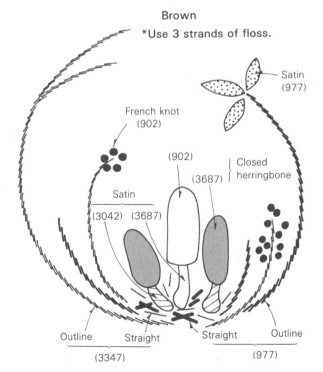

0.6 Bind raw edge with bias tape (see page 67).

11.5

Embroidery area

Overlap ends and turn in raw edge.

Orange
*Use 3 strands of floss.
Work in outline stitch unless otherwise indicated.

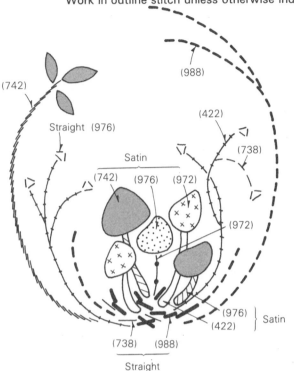

(742)

(988)

Straight (976)

(422)

(738)

Satin
(742) (976) (972)

(972)

(976)
(422) } Satin

(738) (988)

Straight

Brown
*Use 3 strands of floss.

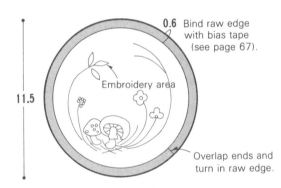

Satin
(977)

French knot
(902)

(902)

(3687)

Closed herringbone

Satin
(3042) (3687)

Outline   Straight   Straight   Outline
(3347)   (977)

Actual size

Yellow-Green
*Use 3 strands of floss.
Work in outline stitch unless otherwise indicated.

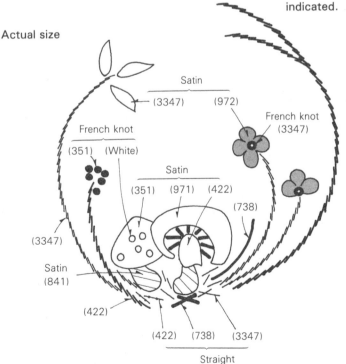

Satin
(3347) (972)

French knot
(3347)

French knot
(351) (White)

Satin
(351) (971) (422)

(738)

(3347)

Satin
(841)

(422)

(422) (738) (3347)

Straight

95

FABRICS: Pink Irish linen, 94cm by 14cm. Pink cotton broadcloth, 64cm by 14cm.
THREADS: DMC 6-strand embroidery floss: small amount each of Peacock Green (991), Scarab Green (3348, 3347), Laurel Green (988), Pistachio Green (368, 367, 320, 319), Emerald Green (912), Umber (739, 738, 436, 435), Beige (3024, 3023), Drab (613), Tangerine Yellow (743, 742, 741), Canary Yellow (972), Geranium Pink (894, 891), Geranium Red (892), Peony Rose (956), Parma Violet (209, 209), Plum (552), Raspberry Red (3689, 3688), Episcopal Purple (718), Flame Red (606), Scarlet (498), Forget-me-not Blue (828, 827, 826), White and Black (310).
NOTIONS: Two-sided iron-on interfacing, 78cm by 14cm. Pink bias tape (1.2cm wide), 170cm. Dowel, 0.5cm in diameter and 14cm long.
FINISHED SIZE: See diagram.

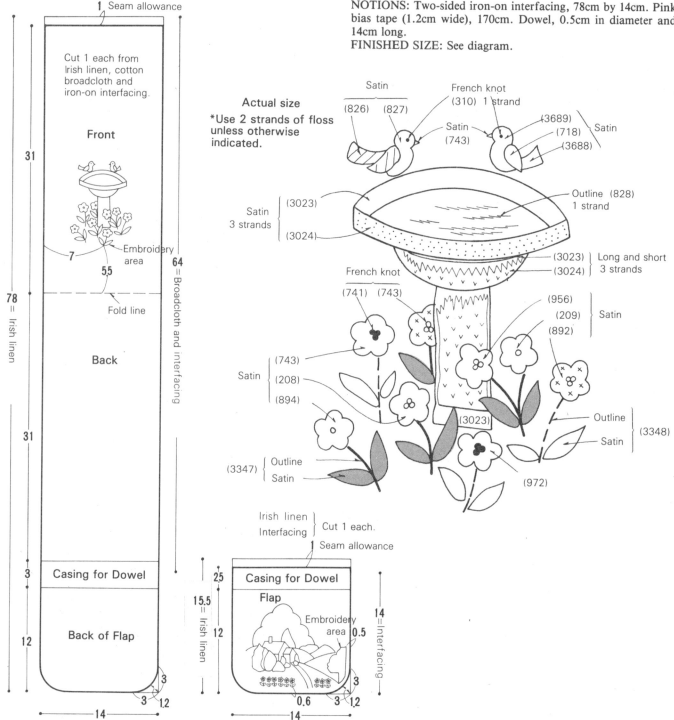

Cut 1 each from Irish linen, cotton broadcloth and iron-on interfacing.

Front

Embroidery area

Fold line

Back

Casing for Dowel

Back of Flap

78 = Irish linen

64 = Broadcloth and interfacing

Seam allowance

Actual size
*Use 2 strands of floss unless otherwise indicated.

Satin (826) (827)

French knot (310) 1 strand

Satin (743)

(3689)
(718)
(3688)
Satin

Outline (828) 1 strand

Satin 3 strands (3023) (3024)

Long and short 3 strands (3023) (3024)

French knot (741) (743)

(956)
(209)
(892)
Satin

Satin (743) (208) (894)

(3023)

Outline
Satin
(3348)

(3347) Outline / Satin

(972)

Irish linen / Interfacing — Cut 1 each.
Seam allowance

Casing for Dowel

Flap

Embroidery area

15.5 = Irish linen

14 = Interfacing

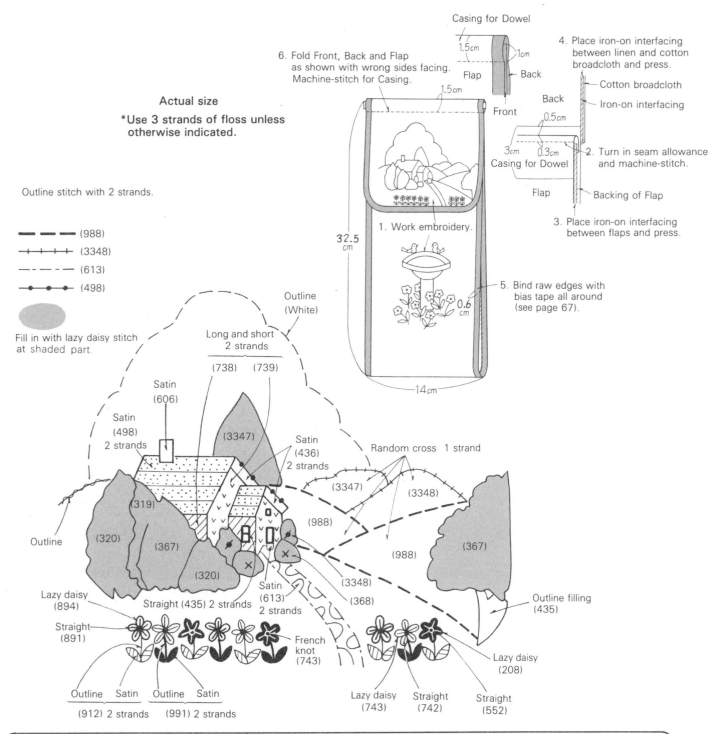

Actual size

*Use 3 strands of floss unless otherwise indicated.

Casing for Dowel

1.5cm | 1cm

Flap — Back

6. Fold Front, Back and Flap as shown with wrong sides facing. Machine-stitch for Casing.

4. Place iron-on interfacing between linen and cotton broadcloth and press.

Cotton broadcloth
Iron-on interfacing

Back

0.5cm

1.5cm

Front

3cm 0.3cm

Casing for Dowel

Flap

2. Turn in seam allowance and machine-stitch.

Backing of Flap

3. Place iron-on interfacing between flaps and press.

1. Work embroidery.

32.5 cm

0.6 cm

5. Bind raw edges with bias tape all around (see page 67).

14cm

Outline stitch with 2 strands.

———— (988)
+++++ (3348)
— · — · — (613)
•—•—•— (498)

Fill in with lazy daisy stitch at shaded part.

Outline (White)

Long and short 2 strands

(738) (739)

Satin (606)

Satin (498) 2 strands

(3347)

Satin (436) 2 strands

Random cross 1 strand

(3347)

(3348)

(319)

(988)

(367)

Outline

(320)

(367)

(367)

(320)

(988)

(988)

(3348)

Satin (613) 2 strands

(368)

Outline filling (435)

Lazy daisy (894)

Straight (435) 2 strands

Straight (891)

French knot (743)

Lazy daisy (208)

Outline Satin

(912) 2 strands

Outline Satin

(991) 2 strands

Lazy daisy (743)

Straight (742)

Straight (552)

Doorknob Cover   Shown on page 40.

MATERIALS FOR ONE
FABRICS: Pink Irish linen, 20cm square. Pink cotton broadcloth, 20cm square.
THREADS: DMC 6-strand embroidery floss:
LEFT---small amount each of Raspberry Red (3685), Episcopal Purple (718), Canary Yellow (972), Tangerine Yellow (743, 741).
RIGHT---small amount each of Forget-me-not Blue (827, 826, 813), Moss Green (472), Scarab Green (3347), Episcopal Purple (718), Parma Violet (211), Plum (553), Geranium Pink (894),

Peony Rose (956), Tangerine Yellow (743), Beaver Gray (648) and Black (310).
NOTIONS: White cotton lace edging (3cm wide), 65cm. Elastic tape (0.5cm wide), 14cm. Light pink satin ribbon (0.9cm wide), 30cm. Bell. Polyester fiberfill. Foam rubber (0.7cm thick), 7cm square.
FINISHED SIZE: See diagram.
DIRECTIONS: Transfer design to linen and embroider. Sew Doorknob Cover as shown.

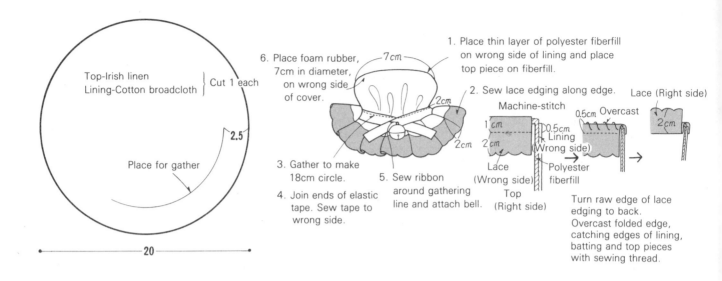

Top-Irish linen
Lining-Cotton broadcloth } Cut 1 each

2.5

Place for gather

20

1. Place thin layer of polyester fiberfill on wrong side of lining and place top piece on fiberfill.

6. Place foam rubber, 7cm in diameter, on wrong side of cover.

7cm

2cm

2cm

2. Sew lace edging along edge. Machine-stitch

Lace (Right side)

2cm

1cm
2cm

0.5cm Overcast

0.5cm

Lining (Wrong side)

Lace (Wrong side)

Polyester fiberfill

Top (Right side)

Turn raw edge of lace edging to back. Overcast folded edge, catching edges of lining, batting and top pieces with sewing thread.

3. Gather to make 18cm circle.

4. Join ends of elastic tape. Sew tape to wrong side.

5. Sew ribbon around gathering line and attach bell.

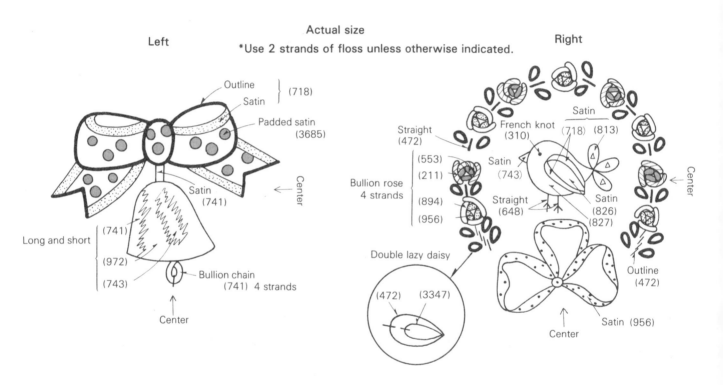

Actual size
*Use 2 strands of floss unless otherwise indicated.

Left

Right

Outline (718)
Satin

Padded satin (3685)

Satin (741)

Center

Long and short { (741)
(972)
(743)

Bullion chain (741) 4 strands

Center

Straight (472)

French knot (310)

Satin (718) (813)

(553)
(211)

Bullion rose 4 strands

(894)
(956)

Satin (743)

Straight (648)

Satin (826) (827)

Center

Outline (472)

Double lazy daisy

(472) (3347)

Satin (956)

Center

T-Shirts   Shown on page 34.

BICYCLE
MATERIALS: White T-Shirt. Scraps of cotton fabric, Beige and Red.
THREADS: DMC 6-strand embroidery floss:
small amount each of Poppy (666), Ash Gray (318, 317), Pistachio Green (319), Lemon Yellow (445).
DIRECTIONS: Transfer design to center top of T-shirt and embroider.

FLOWER BOUQUET
MATERIAL: White T-Shirt.
THREADS: DMC 6-strand embroidery floss:
1/2 skein each of Pistachio Green (320), Forget-me-not Blue (824); small amount each of Cerise (603, 601), Magenta Rose (963), Geranium Pink (894), Emerald Green (912), Brilliant Green (699), Forget-me-not Blue (827, 825), Royal Blue (820), Saffron (727), Lemon Yellow (445), Cornflower Blue (793) and Plum (554, 552).
DIRECTIONS: Transfer design to left top of T-shirt and embroider.

Actual size   *Use 3 strands of floss unless otherwise indicated.

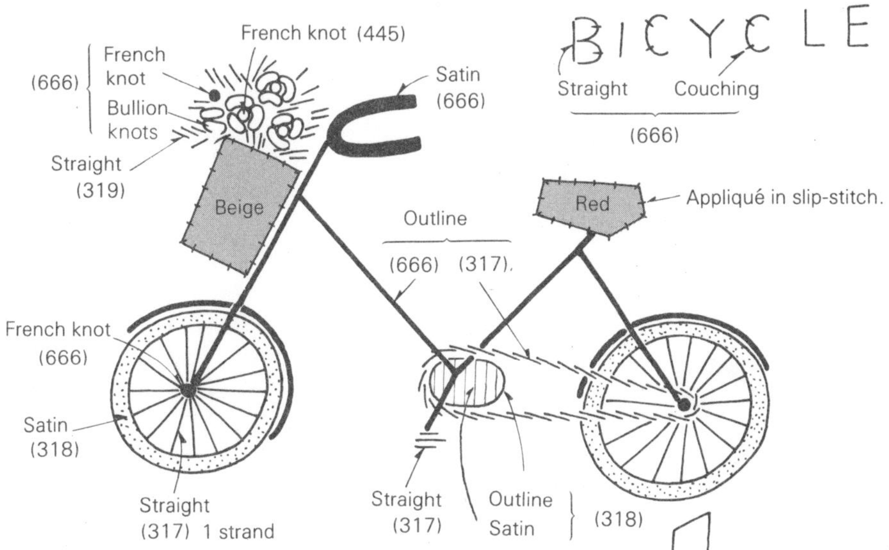

French knot (445)

(666) { French knot / Bullion knots

Straight (319)

Satin (666)

Beige

B I C Y C L E

Straight   Couching

(666)

Red — Appliqué in slip-stitch.

Outline

(666)   (317)

French knot (666)

Satin (318)

Straight (317) 1 strand

Straight (317)

Outline Satin } (318)

Actual size   *Use 3 strands of floss.

a = 963
b = 894
c = 603
d = 320 } Satin

Outline filling (820)

Outline (320)

Satin (824)

(445) { Satin / French knot

French knot (601)

French knot filling (793)

(727)

(699) } Outline

(912)

French knot (820)

Satin (827)

Outline filling (825)

Straight { (554) / (552)

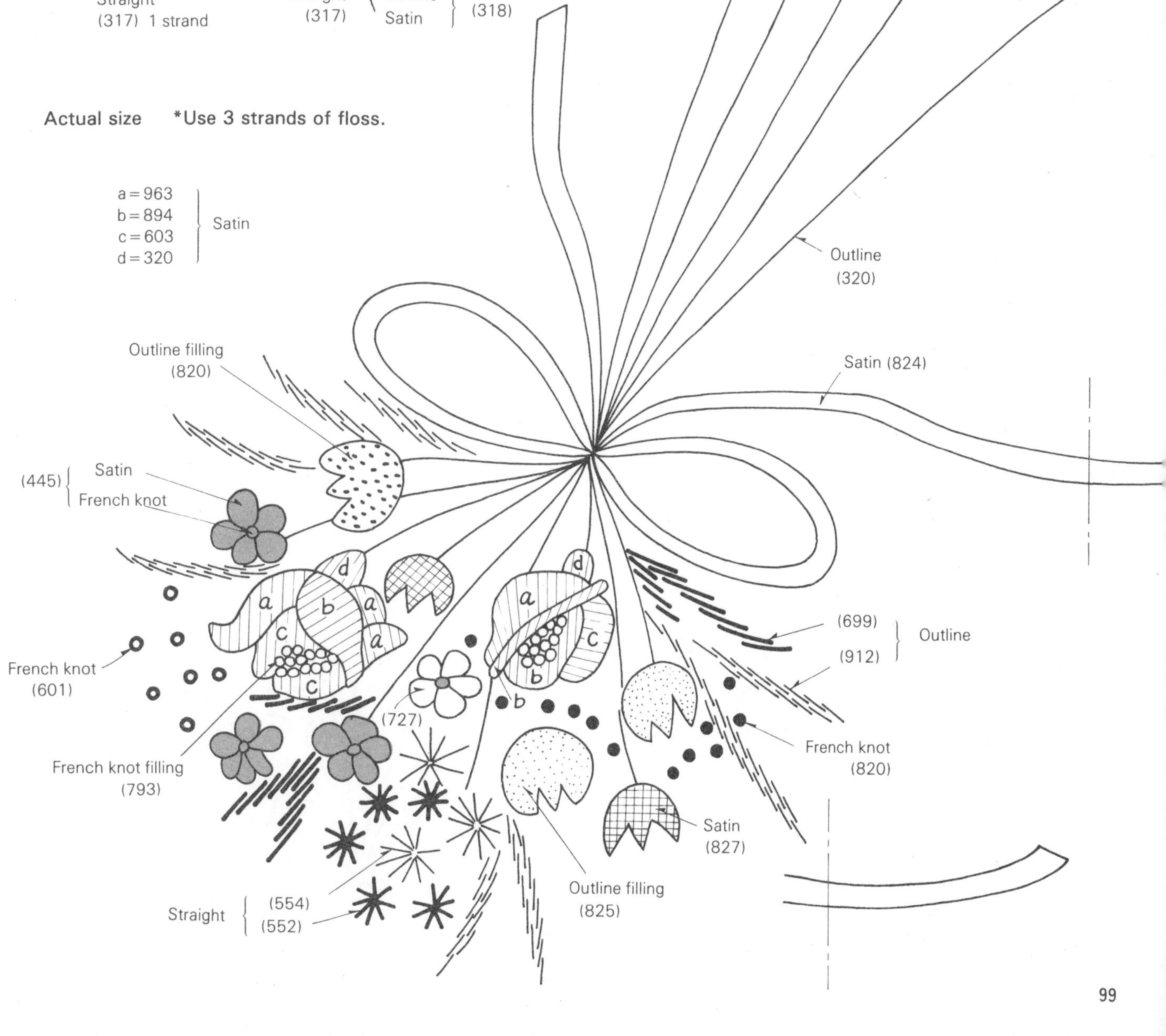

Village Bedspread   Shown on pages 32 and 33.

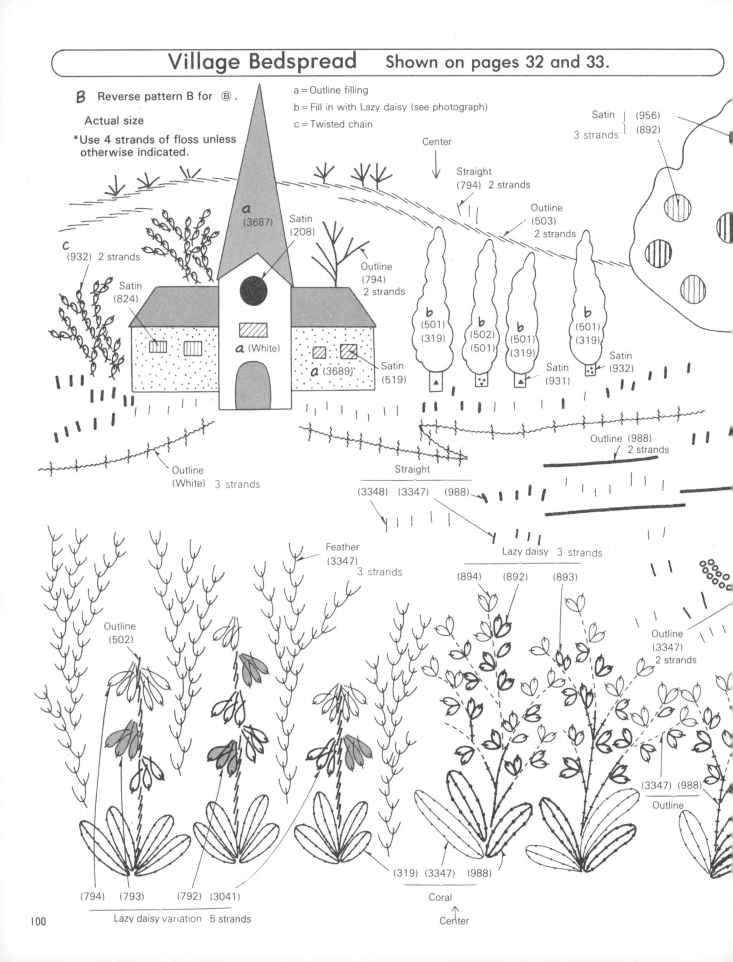

B Reverse pattern B for Ⓑ.

Actual size

*Use 4 strands of floss unless otherwise indicated.

a = Outline filling
b = Fill in with Lazy daisy (see photograph)
c = Twisted chain

Center

Straight (794) 2 strands

Outline (503) 2 strands

Satin (956) (892) 3 strands

a (3687)

Satin (208)

Outline (794) 2 strands

c (932) 2 strands

Satin (824)

b (501) (319)

b (502) (501)

b (501) (319)

b (501) (319)

a (White)

a (3689)

Satin (519)

Satin (931)

Satin (932)

Outline (White) 3 strands

Outline (988) 2 strands

Straight

(3348)   (3347)   (988)

Lazy daisy 3 strands

(894)   (892)   (893)

Feather (3347) 3 strands

Outline (3347) 2 strands

Outline (502)

(3347) (988)

Outline

(319) (3347) (988)

(794)   (793)   (792) (3041)

Lazy daisy variation 5 strands

Coral

Center

100

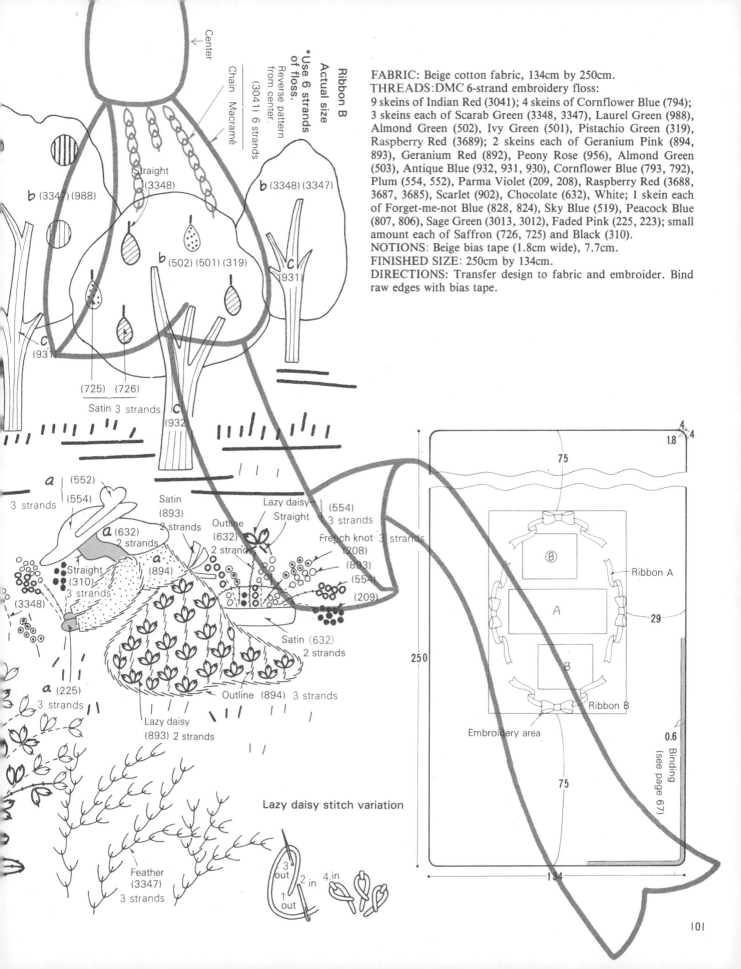

Center

Ribbon B
Actual size
*Use 6 strands of floss.

Reverse pattern from center.
(3041) 6 strands

Chain Macramé

Straight
(3348)

b (3347) (988)

b (3348) (3347)

b (502) (501) (319)

C (931)

C (931)

C (932)

(725)   (726)

Satin 3 strands

a (552)
(554)
3 strands

Satin
(893)
2 strands

Outline
(632)
2 strands

Lazy daisy
Straight

(554)
3 strands

a (632)
2 strands

a (894)

Straight
(310)
3 strands

French knot 3 strands
(208)

(893)

(554)

(209)

(3348)

Satin (632)
2 strands

a (225)
3 strands

Outline (894) 3 strands

Lazy daisy
(893) 2 strands

Feather
(3347)
3 strands

Lazy daisy stitch variation

3 out
2 in
1 out
4 in

FABRIC: Beige cotton fabric, 134cm by 250cm.
THREADS:DMC 6-strand embroidery floss:
9 skeins of Indian Red (3041); 4 skeins of Cornflower Blue (794);
3 skeins each of Scarab Green (3348, 3347), Laurel Green (988),
Almond Green (502), Ivy Green (501), Pistachio Green (319),
Raspberry Red (3689); 2 skeins each of Geranium Pink (894,
893), Geranium Red (892), Peony Rose (956), Almond Green
(503), Antique Blue (932, 931, 930), Cornflower Blue (793, 792),
Plum (554, 552), Parma Violet (209, 208), Raspberry Red (3688,
3687, 3685), Scarlet (902), Chocolate (632), White; 1 skein each
of Forget-me-not Blue (828, 824), Sky Blue (519), Peacock Blue
(807, 806), Sage Green (3013, 3012), Faded Pink (225, 223); small
amount each of Saffron (726, 725) and Black (310).
NOTIONS: Beige bias tape (1.8cm wide), 7.7cm.
FINISHED SIZE: 250cm by 134cm.
DIRECTIONS: Transfer design to fabric and embroider. Bind
raw edges with bias tape.

4
4
1.8

75

B

A

Ribbon A

29

B

250

Ribbon B

Embroidery area

75

0.6

Binding
(see page 67)

134

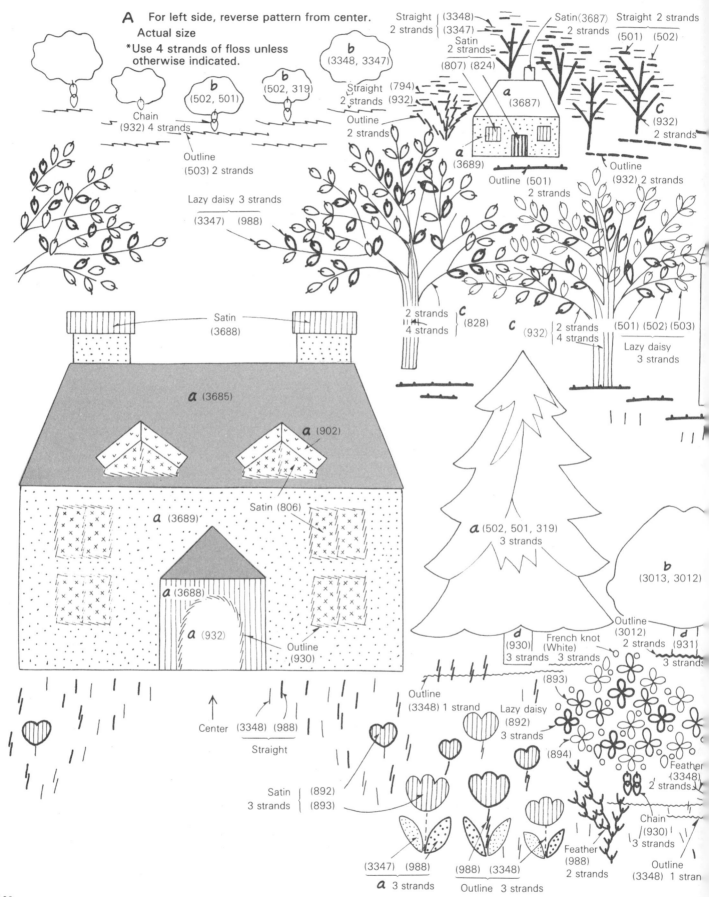

A For left side, reverse pattern from center.
Actual size
*Use 4 strands of floss unless otherwise indicated.

b
(3348, 3347)

b
(502, 501)

b
(502, 319)

Chain
(932) 4 strands

Outline
(503) 2 strands

Lazy daisy 3 strands
(3347) (988)

Straight
2 strands (3348)
(3347)

Satin
2 strands
(807) (824)

Satin (3687)
2 strands

Straight 2 strands
(501) (502)

Straight
2 strands (794)
(932)

Outline
2 strands

a
(3687)

a
(3689)

a

Outline (501)
2 strands

c
(932)

Outline
(932) 2 strands

Satin
(3688)

a (3685)

a (902)

Satin (806)

a (3689)

a (3688)

a (932)

Outline
(930)

2 strands
4 strands

c
(828)

c
(932)
2 strands
4 strands

(501) (502) (503)
Lazy daisy
3 strands

a (502, 501, 319)
3 strands

b
(3013, 3012)

Outline
(3012)
2 strands

d
(931)
3 strands

d
(930)
3 strands

French knot
(White)
3 strands

(893)

Lazy daisy
(892)
3 strands

Feather
(3348)
2 strands

Center
(3348) (988)
Straight

Outline
(3348) 1 strand

(894)

Satin (892)
3 strands (893)

(3347) (988)
a 3 strands

(988) (3348)
Outline 3 strands

Feather
(988)
2 strands

Chain
(930)
3 strands

Outline
(3348) 1 stran

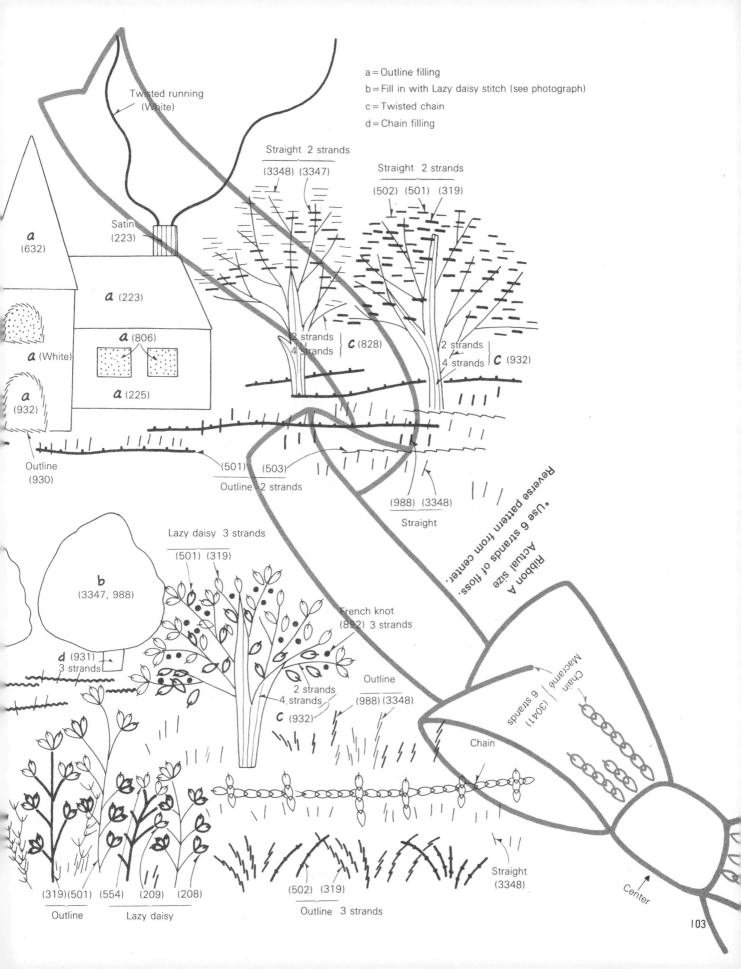

a = Outline filling
b = Fill in with Lazy daisy stitch (see photograph)
c = Twisted chain
d = Chain filling

Twisted running
(White)

Satin
(223)

a
(632)

a (223)

a (806)

a (White)

a (225)

a
(932)

Outline
(930)

Straight 2 strands
(3348) (3347)

Straight 2 strands
(502) (501) (319)

2 strands
4 strands } *c* (828)

2 strands
4 strands } *c* (932)

(501) (503)
Outline 2 strands

(988) (3348)
Straight

*Use 6 strands of floss.
Reverse pattern from center.
Actual size
Ribbon A

Lazy daisy 3 strands
(501) (319)

b
(3347, 988)

French knot
(892) 3 strands

d (931)
3 strands

2 strands
4 strands

Outline
(988) (3348)

c (932)

Chain
Macramé } (3041) 6 strands

Chain

Center

(319) (501) (554) (209) (208)
Outline   Lazy daisy

(502) (319)
Outline 3 strands

Straight
(3348)

103

FRUIT BASKET
MATERIAL: Apron.
THREADS: DMC 6-strand embroidery floss:
1/2 skein each of Peony Rose (956), Geranium Red (892), Brilliant Green (702), Canary Yellow (971), Fire Red (947),
Tangerine Yellow (741, 740), Parma Violet (209), Umber (433); small amount each of Scarab Green (3348, 3347).
DIRECTIONS: Transfer design to center top and pocket of apron and embroider.

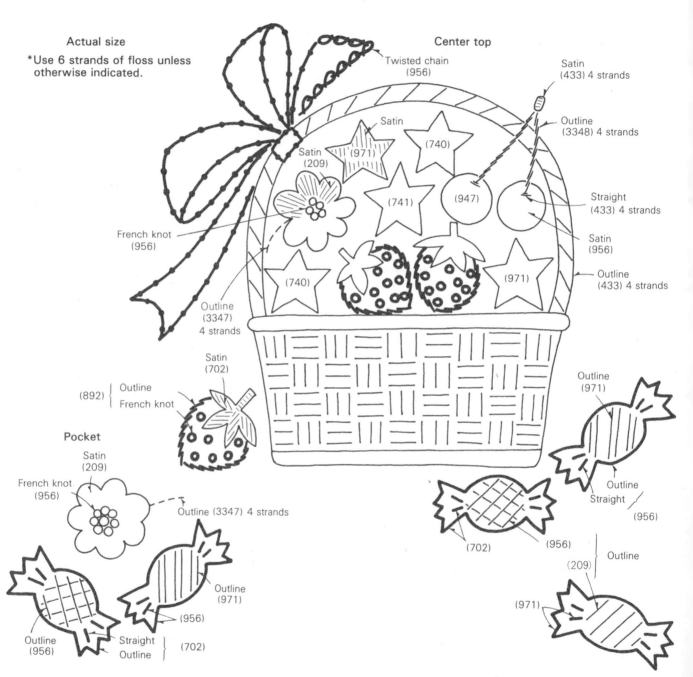

Actual size

*Use 6 strands of floss unless otherwise indicated.

Center top

Twisted chain (956)

Satin (433) 4 strands

Satin (971)

Satin (209)

Satin (740)

Outline (3348) 4 strands

French knot (956)

(741)

(947)

Straight (433) 4 strands

Satin (956)

Outline (433) 4 strands

(740)

(971)

Outline (3347) 4 strands

Satin (702)

Satin (702)

(892) { Outline
       French knot

Pocket

Satin (209)

French knot (956)

Outline (3347) 4 strands

Outline (971)

Outline (971)

Outline Straight

(956)

(702)   (956)

(209) } Outline

Outline (956)

Outline (971)

(956)

(971)

Outline (956)

Straight Outline } (702)

DOLLS
MATERIAL: Apron.
THREADS: DMC 6-strand embroidery floss:
1 skein of Forget-me-not Blue (827); 1/2 skein each of Scarlet (902), Saffron (725), Golden Yellow (783), Cornflower Blue (794, 792), Parma Violet (209), Plum (552); small amount each of
Geranium Red (352), Cardinal Red (347), Azure Blue (3325), Forget-me-not Blue (826), Hazelnut Brown (422) and Beige Brown (841).
DIRECTIONS: Transfer design to center top of apron and embroider.

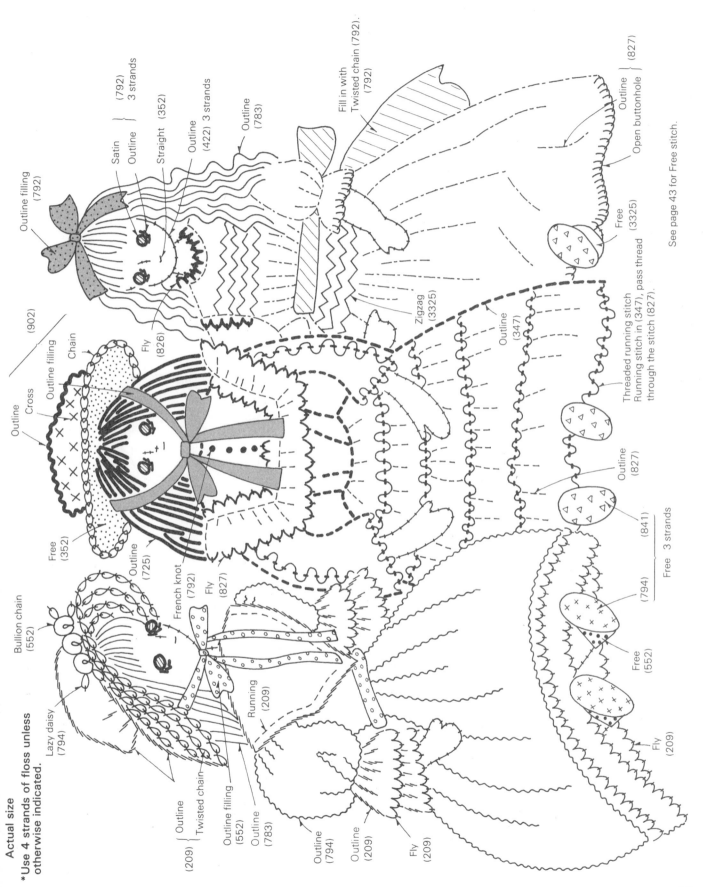

Actual size

*Use 4 strands of floss unless otherwise indicated.

Outline filling (792)

Satin (792) 3 strands
Outline
Straight (352)
Outline (422) 3 strands
Outline (783)

Fill in with Twisted chain (792).

Outline (827)
Open buttonhole

Free (3325)

See page 43 for Free stitch.

Zigzag (3325)

Outline (347)

Threaded running stitch
Running stitch in (347), pass thread through the stitch (827).

Cross (902)
Outline filling
Outline
Chain
Fly (826)

Outline (827)

Free (352)
Outline (725)

French knot (792)
Fly (827)

Outline (841)

Free (794) 3 strands

Free (552)

Fly (209)

Bullion chain (552)

Lazy daisy (794)

Outline (209)
Twisted chain
Outline filling (552)
Outline (783)

Running (209)

Outline (794)
Outline (209)
Fly (209)
Fly (209)

105

BIRTHDAY CAKE
MATERIAL: Apron.
THREADS: DMC
6-strand embroidery
floss:
1-1/2 skeins each of
Soft Pink (776),
Cerise (603); 1/2 skein
each of Cerise (605,
604, 602), Almond
Green (503), Azure
Blue (3325), Canary
Yellow (972); small
amount of Seagull
Gray (451).
DIRECTIONS:
Transfer design to
center top of apron
and embroider.

Actual size
*Use 4 strands of floss unless
otherwise indicated.
See page 43 for Free stitch.

Satin (972) 3 strands

Straight (451)

Outline filling
(3325)

Free
(502)
3 strands

(604)
(603)   } Free 3 strands
(776)

(603)   } Satin 3 strands
(776)

Lazy daisy   } (604)
Outline   } 3 strands

Outline
(776)

Chain
(603)

Twisted chain
(776)

Cable
(604)

Couched trellis (605)

Outline
(776)

Outline (603)

Outline
(604)

Lazy daisy
(604)

Happy Birthday

(602) } Outline
(603)

Fly
(605)

Open buttonhole
(3325)

106

Tissue Box Cover   Shown on page 38.

FABRICS: Yellow-Green Java canvas (35 threads to 10cm), 84cm by 21cm. Cotton fabric for lining, 84cm by 19cm.
THREADS: Anchor 6-strand embroidery floss:
1 skein each of Morocco Red (9), Geranium Red (11), Tangerine Yellow (297, 298); 1/2 skein each of Geranium Red (10), Green (262), Parakeet Green (257), Copper Green (856), Drab (375); small amount each of Geranium Red (6), Mahogany (352) and White.

NOTIONS: Elastic tape (0.7cm wide), 12cm.
FINISHED SIZE: See diagram.
DIRECTIONS: Cross-stitch as indicated. Sew Tissue Box Cover following diagram.

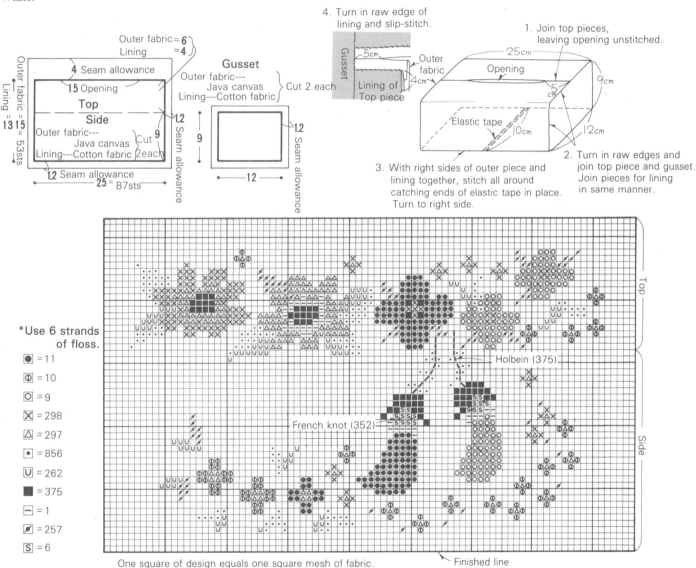

One square of design equals one square mesh of fabric.

*Use 6 strands of floss.

◉ = 11
Φ = 10
○ = 9
✕ = 298
△ = 297
• = 856
U = 262
■ = 375
― = 1
⟋ = 257
S = 6

Cosmetic Bag   Shown on page 38.

FABRICS: Blue Irish linen, 32cm by 27cm. Cotton fabric for lining, 32cm by 17cm.
THREADS: Anchor 6-strand embroidery floss:
1/2 skein each of Plum (98), Parma Violet (110), Moss Green (267); small amount of Canary Yellow (302).

FINISHED SIZE: See diagram.
DIRECTIONS: Transfer design to fabric, placing flower motifs as shown in diagram. Embroider. Sew Cosmetic Bag following diagram.

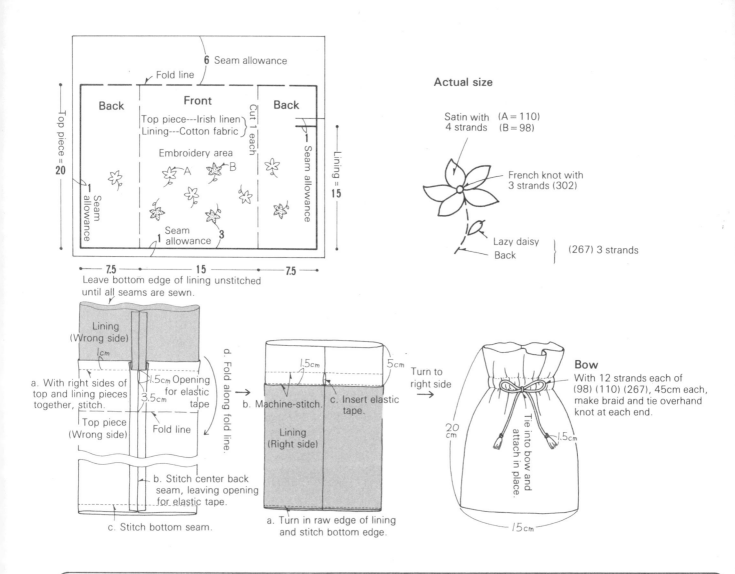

6 Seam allowance

Fold line

Back   Front   Back

Top piece---Irish linen
Lining---Cotton fabric

Embroidery area

A   B

1 Seam allowance

Cut 1 each

Top piece = 20

1 Seam allowance

Lining = 15

1 Seam allowance

3

Seam allowance

7.5   15   7.5

Leave bottom edge of lining unstitched until all seams are sewn.

Actual size

Satin with 4 strands   (A = 110) (B = 98)

French knot with 3 strands (302)

Lazy daisy
Back

(267) 3 strands

Lining (Wrong side)

1cm

a. With right sides of top and lining pieces together, stitch.

1.5cm Opening for elastic tape

3.5cm

Top piece (Wrong side)

Fold line

d. Fold along fold line.

b. Stitch center back seam, leaving opening for elastic tape.

c. Stitch bottom seam.

1.5cm   5cm

Turn to right side

b. Machine-stitch.

c. Insert elastic tape.

Lining (Right side)

a. Turn in raw edge of lining and stitch bottom edge.

Bow
With 12 strands each of (98) (110) (267), 45cm each, make braid and tie overhand knot at each end.

Tie into bow and attach in place.

20 cm

1.5cm

15cm

Tissue Case and Matching Cosmetic Case   Shown on page 38.

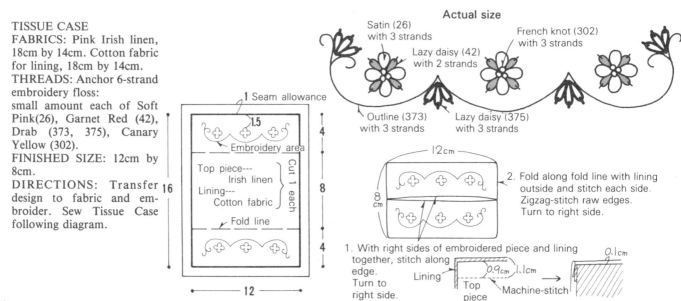

TISSUE CASE
FABRICS: Pink Irish linen, 18cm by 14cm. Cotton fabric for lining, 18cm by 14cm.
THREADS: Anchor 6-strand embroidery floss:
small amount each of Soft Pink(26), Garnet Red (42), Drab (373, 375), Canary Yellow (302).
FINISHED SIZE: 12cm by 8cm.
DIRECTIONS: Transfer design to fabric and embroider. Sew Tissue Case following diagram.

Actual size

Satin (26) with 3 strands

Lazy daisy (42) with 2 strands

French knot (302) with 3 strands

Outline (373) with 3 strands

Lazy daisy (375) with 3 strands

1 Seam allowance

1.5

Embroidery area

Top piece--- Irish linen

Lining--- Cotton fabric

Fold line

Cut 1 each

16

4

8

4

12

12cm

8 cm

2. Fold along fold line with lining outside and stitch each side. Zigzag-stitch raw edges. Turn to right side.

1. With right sides of embroidered piece and lining together, stitch along edge. Turn to right side.

Lining

Top piece

0.9cm   1.1cm

Machine-stitch

0.1cm

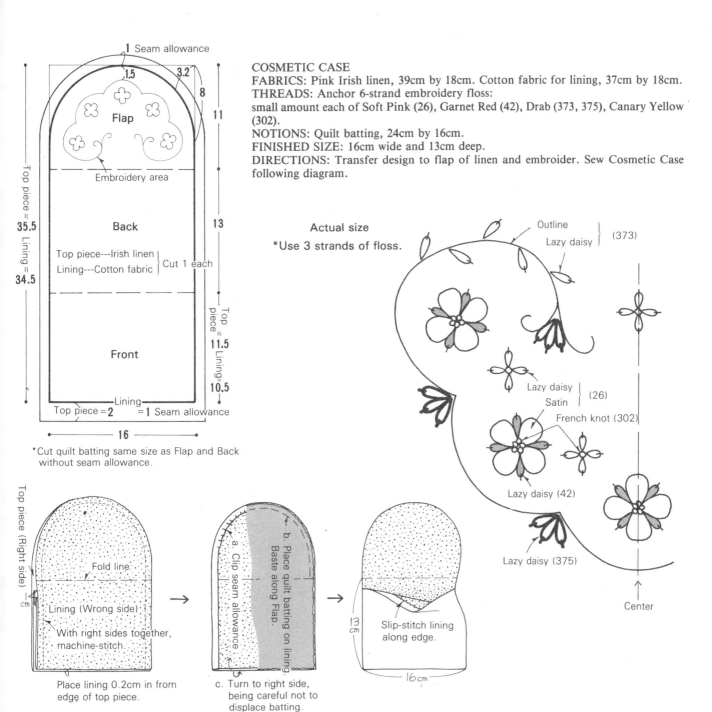

COSMETIC CASE

FABRICS: Pink Irish linen, 39cm by 18cm. Cotton fabric for lining, 37cm by 18cm.
THREADS: Anchor 6-strand embroidery floss:
small amount each of Soft Pink (26), Garnet Red (42), Drab (373, 375), Canary Yellow (302).
NOTIONS: Quilt batting, 24cm by 16cm.
FINISHED SIZE: 16cm wide and 13cm deep.
DIRECTIONS: Transfer design to flap of linen and embroider. Sew Cosmetic Case following diagram.

Actual size
*Use 3 strands of floss.

Figure labels (pattern, left):
1 Seam allowance
1.5   3.2
8
11
Flap
Embroidery area
Back
13
Top piece---Irish linen
Lining---Cotton fabric } Cut 1 each
Top piece = 35.5 / Lining = 34.5
Top piece = 11.5 / Lining = 10.5
Front
Lining
Top piece = 2 = 1 Seam allowance
16

*Cut quilt batting same size as Flap and Back without seam allowance.

Embroidery diagram labels:
Outline
Lazy daisy } (373)
Lazy daisy } (26)
Satin
French knot (302)
Lazy daisy (42)
Lazy daisy (375)
Center

Construction diagram labels:
Top piece (Right side)
Fold line
Lining (Wrong side)
With right sides together, machine-stitch.
Place lining 0.2cm in from edge of top piece.
a. Clip seam allowance
b. Place quilt batting on lining. Baste along Flap.
c. Turn to right side, being careful not to displace batting.
13 cm
Slip-stitch lining along edge.
16 cm

Tote Bags   Shown on page 39.

TOTE BAG, TOP

FABRICS: Olive-Green Irish linen, 26cm by 19cm. Ash-Brown quilted fabric, 84cm by 47cm. Cotton fabric for lining, 77cm by 42cm.
THREADS: DMC 6-strand embroidery floss:
3 skeins of Laurel Green (988); 1 skein each of Laurel Green (986), Saffron (726, 725), White, Sky Blue (517); 1/2 skein each of Emerald Green (911), Peacock Green (992), Scarab Green (3348, 3347), Parakeet Green (904), Sky Blue (518), Saffron(727), Golden Yellow (783), Tangerine Yellow (741, 740), Canary Yellow (970), Parma Violet (210, 209) and Plum (554).
NOTIONS: 4 self-covered buttons, 2.5cm in diameter. Elastic tape (0.6cm wide), 14cm.
FINISHED SIZE: 40cm wide and 33cm deep.

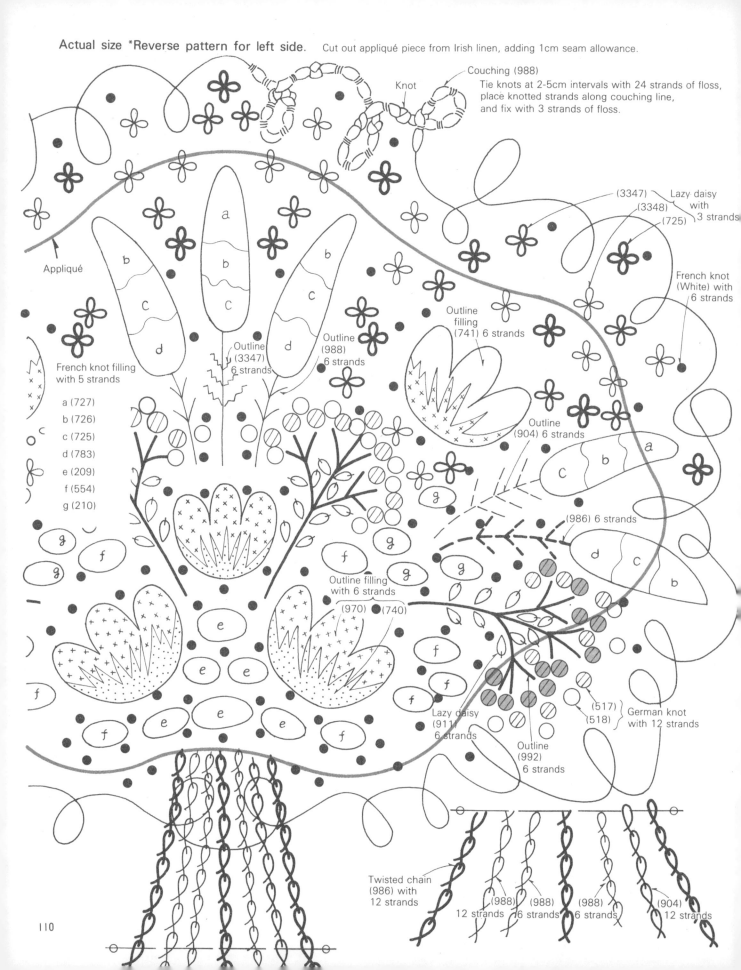

Actual size *Reverse pattern for left side. Cut out appliqué piece from Irish linen, adding 1cm seam allowance.

Couching (988)
Tie knots at 2-5cm intervals with 24 strands of floss,
place knotted strands along couching line,
and fix with 3 strands of floss.

Knot

(3347) Lazy daisy
(3348) with
(725) 3 strands

Appliqué

French knot
(White) with
6 strands

a
b
b
b
c
c
c
d
d

Outline filling
(741) 6 strands

Outline
(3347)
6 strands

Outline
(988)
6 strands

Outline
(904) 6 strands

a
b
c

French knot filling
with 5 strands

a (727)
b (726)
c (725)
d (783)
e (209)
f (554)
g (210)

g

d
c
b

(986) 6 strands

g
f

g

g

f
g
g

Outline filling
with 6 strands
(970) (740)

e

f

f
f

(517)
(518)

German knot
with 12 strands

e
e

f

e
e

e

f

Lazy daisy
(911)
6 strands

Outline
(992)
6 strands

Twisted chain
(986) with
12 strands

(988)
12 strands

(988)
6 strands

(988)
6 strands

(904)
12 strands

110

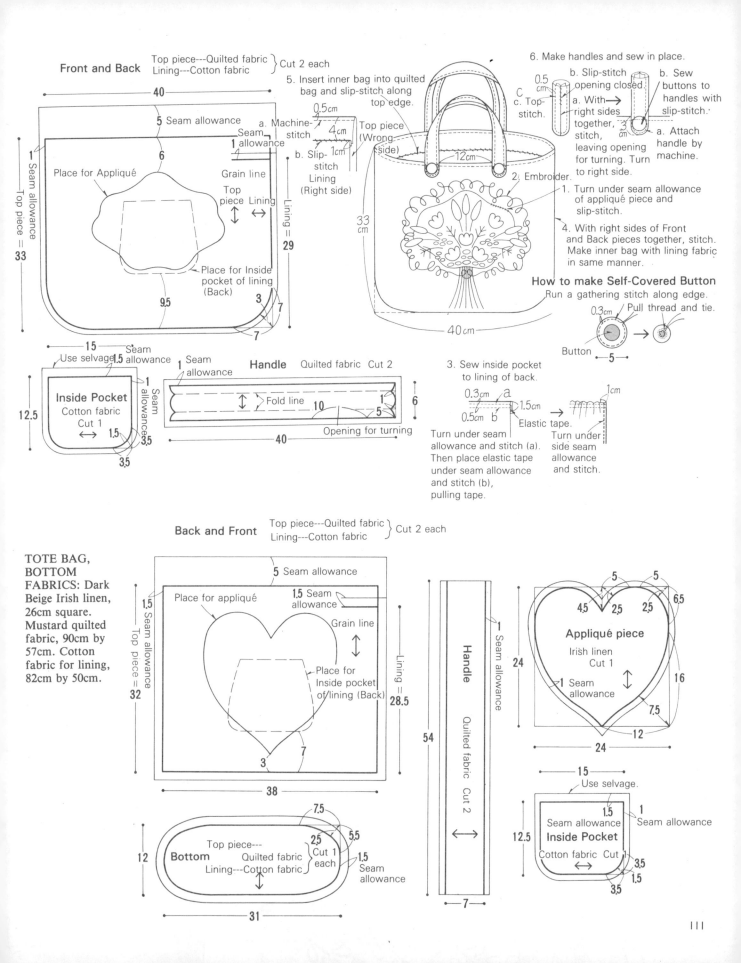

Front and Back Top piece---Quilted fabric / Lining---Cotton fabric } Cut 2 each

40

5 Seam allowance

1 Seam allowance

1 Seam allowance

6

Place for Appliqué

Grain line

Top piece ↕ Lining ↔

Lining =

29

33

Top piece =

Place for Inside pocket of lining (Back)

9.5

3

7

7

15

Use selvage. 1.5 Seam allowance

1 Seam allowance

Inside Pocket
Cotton fabric
Cut 1

12.5

1.5

3.5

3.5

Seam allowance

Handle Quilted fabric Cut 2

1 Seam allowance

↕ Fold line

10

1

5

6

Opening for turning

5. Insert inner bag into quilted bag and slip-stitch along top edge.

0.5cm

4cm

1cm

a. Machine-stitch

b. Slip-stitch

Top piece (Wrong side)

Lining (Right side)

12cm

33 cm

2. Embroider.

40 cm

6. Make handles and sew in place.

0.5 cm

C

b. Slip-stitch opening closed.

a. With right sides together, stitch, leaving opening for turning. Turn to right side.

c. Top-stitch.

b. Sew buttons to handles with slip-stitch.

3 cm

a. Attach handle by machine.

1. Turn under seam allowance of appliqué piece and slip-stitch.

4. With right sides of Front and Back pieces together, stitch. Make inner bag with lining fabric in same manner.

How to make Self-Covered Button
Run a gathering stitch along edge.

0.3cm Pull thread and tie.

Button

5

3. Sew inside pocket to lining of back.

0.3cm a
0.5cm b

1.5cm

Elastic tape.

1cm

Turn under seam allowance and stitch (a). Then place elastic tape under seam allowance and stitch (b), pulling tape.

Turn under side seam allowance and stitch.

Back and Front Top piece---Quilted fabric / Lining---Cotton fabric } Cut 2 each

TOTE BAG, BOTTOM FABRICS: Dark Beige Irish linen, 26cm square. Mustard quilted fabric, 90cm by 57cm. Cotton fabric for lining, 82cm by 50cm.

5 Seam allowance

1.5

Place for appliqué

1.5 Seam allowance

Grain line ↕

Top piece =

Seam allowance

32

Place for Inside pocket of lining (Back)

Lining =

28.5

3

7

38

7.5

2.5

5.5

12

Bottom Top piece--- Quilted fabric / Lining---Cotton fabric } Cut 1 each

1.5 Seam allowance

31

Handle

Quilted fabric Cut 2

1 Seam allowance

54

↔

7

5

5

4.5 2.5 2.5 6.5

Appliqué piece
Irish linen
Cut 1

24

1 Seam allowance

16

7.5

12

24

15

Use selvage.

1.5

1 Seam allowance

12.5

Inside Pocket
Cotton fabric Cut 1

Seam allowance

↔

3.5

1.5

3.5

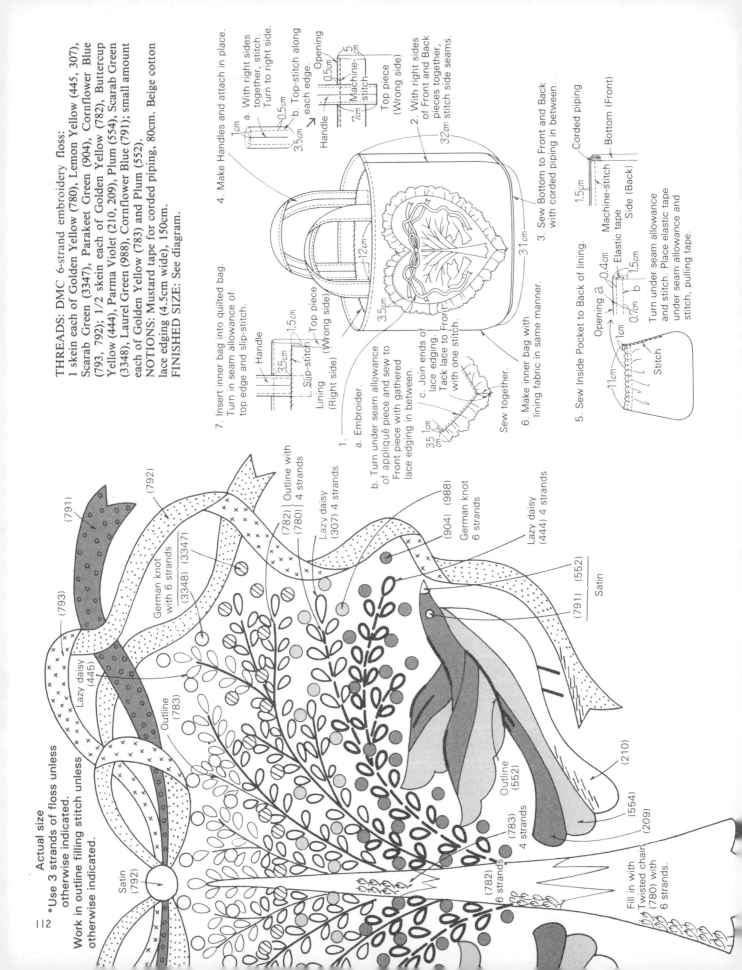

THREADS: DMC 6-strand embroidery floss:
1 skein each of Golden Yellow (780), Lemon Yellow (445, 307), Scarab Green (3347), Parakeet Green (904), Cornflower Blue (793, 792); 1/2 skein each of Golden Yellow (782), Buttercup Yellow (444), Parma Violet (210, 209), Plum (554), Scarab Green (3348), Laurel Green (988), Cornflower Blue (791); small amount each of Golden Yellow (783) and Plum (552).
NOTIONS: Mustard tape for corded piping, 80cm. Beige cotton lace edging (4.5cm wide), 150cm.
FINISHED SIZE: See diagram.

4. Make Handles and attach in place.
a. With right sides together, stitch. Turn to right side.
b. Top-stitch along each edge.
Handle — 1cm, 3.5cm, 0.5cm
Machine-stitch, Opening, 5cm, 7cm, 0.5cm
Top piece (Wrong side)

2. With right sides of Front and Back pieces together, stitch side seams. — 32cm

3. Sew Bottom to Front and Back with corded piping in between.
Corded piping, Bottom (Front), 1.5cm, Machine-stitch, Side (Back), 31cm, 3.5cm, 12cm

1.
a. Embroider.
b. Turn under seam allowance of appliqué piece and sew to Front piece with gathered lace edging in between.
c. Join ends of lace edging. Tack lace to Front with one stitch.
Sew together. 3.5cm, 1cm

6. Make inner bag with lining fabric in same manner.

5. Sew Inside Pocket to Back of lining.
Opening, 0.4cm, Elastic tape, 1.5cm, 0.7cm, 1cm, 11cm, Stitch.
Turn under seam allowance and stitch. Place elastic tape under seam allowance and stitch, pulling tape.

7. Insert inner bag into quilted bag. Turn in seam allowance of top edge and slip-stitch.
Handle, 1.5cm, 3.5cm, Top piece, Slip-stitch, Lining (Right side), Top piece (Wrong side)

Actual size
*Use 3 strands of floss unless otherwise indicated.
Work in outline filling stitch unless otherwise indicated.

(791)
(792)
(793)
Satin (792)
Lazy daisy (445)
Outline (783)
German knot with 6 strands
(3348) (3347)
(782) (780) Outline with 4 strands
Lazy daisy (307) 4 strands
(904) (988) German knot 6 strands
Lazy daisy (444) 4 strands
(791) (552) Satin
(210)
Outline (552)
(554)
(209)
(782) 6 strands
(783) 4 strands
Fill in with Twisted chain (780) with 6 strands.